Alex Murray/.50

NUMIS

A LANGUAGE OF ITS OWN

KEY DEFINITIONS IN
NUMISMATICS

JAMES MACKAY

Frederick Muller Limited
London

First published in Great Britain 1982
by Frederick Muller Limited, London SW19 7JU

British Library Cataloguing in Publication Data

Mackay, James
    Key definitions in numismatics. — (A Language of its own)
    1. Numismatics — Dictionaries
    I. Title   II. Series
737'.03'21   CJ67

ISBN 0-584 11017-0

This book is set in 10/11½ point VIP Sabon by
D. P. Media Limited, Hitchin, Hertfordshire
Printed in Great Britain by
Redwood Burn Ltd.
Trowbridge, Wiltshire

Preface

The Latin word for a coin (*numisma*) has given us the word numismatics to denote the study of coins and medals. The tremendous growth of numismatics in the present century has been accompanied by diversification into related subjects – tokens and metal tickets, orders, military medals and decorations, and, most recent of all, banknotes, bills of exchange, promissory notes, cheques and other forms of paper money.

Like other branches of learning, numismatics has developed a language of its own. A relatively small number of terms relate to the anatomy of coins, medals and tokens, or to the methods of their production, and such expressions as obverse and reverse, pile and trussel, brockage and mis-strike, soon become familiar to the numismatist. On the other hand, numismatics yields a vast and bewildering array of the names given to coins over a period spanning almost 28 centuries. This is a trend that shows no signs of diminishing. No longer are the traditional dollar and cent sufficient to meet the needs of emergent nations and, in a bid to assert their individuality, they must adopt monetary systems whose units have more and more exotic names. The butut, licente, lilangeni, ngwee, sylis and tambala are but a few of the coins to emerge in recent years.

Space prevents the inclusion of popular nicknames such as bob and buck, tanner and tickey, but many coins, including the gold sovereign of the present day, are known by names that do not appear on them, and there must be numerous borderline cases. The criterion for inclusion is the name by which a coin is known to numismatists.

For Nita and David Savage

A

Abbasi (abbassi, abasi, abaze). Silver coin first struck in the reign of Shah Abbas I (1587–1629) after whom it was named. In Persia 4 **shahis** = 1 abbasi and 50 abbasis = 1 **toman.** From 1762 abbasis were struck in Georgia (5 abbasis = 1 **rouble**).

Abschlag (German) Restrike from an original die.

Ackey Silver coin worth 8 **tackoe** struck by the British African Company for circulation in the Gold Coast between 1796 and 1818, and based on an ancient Ashanti unit of gold weight.

Acmonital Acronym from A*c*iaio *Mon*etario *Ital*iano, a nickel alloy adopted for Italian coins in 1939 as a substitute for silver.

Ae. Abbreviation for the Latin *Aes* (bronze) used for coins made of brass, bronze or other copper alloys.

Aes Grave (Latin for heavy bronze) Heavy circular coins first minted by Rome in 269 B.C.

Aes Rude (Latin for rough bronze) Irregular lumps of bronze which gradually developed into ingots of uniform shape and were the precursors of coins in Rome.

Aes Signatum (Latin for signed bronze) Bronze ingots of regular size and weight, bearing marks of authority to guarantee their weight and used between 289 B.C. and 269 B.C.

Afghani Unit of currency adopted by Afghanistan in 1926. 100 **puls** = 1 afghani; 20 afghanis = 1 **amani**.

Agnel (agnelete, agnelot)   Alternative names for the French mouton d'or, from the Latin *Agnus Dei* (Lamb of God).

Agora (plural **agorot**)   Israeli unit of currency since 1963. 100 agorot = 1 **lira** or Israeli pound.

Alloy   Coinage metal composed of two or more metallic elements.

Altun   Turkish gold coin introduced by Muhammed II in 1454, modelled on the **ducat** and **zecchino** of Italy.

Altyn   Originally money of account in Russia (from the Tatar word *alty* meaning "six"), it was eventually used as the name for a silver coin worth 6 denga, struck in the second half of the 17th century. Following the currency reforms of Peter the Great in 1698 the altyn became a 3-kopek coin. The name was retained for the copper 3-kopek coins of the 19th century and the aluminium bronze coins of the Soviet period were known by the diminutive form **altynnik**. The 15-kopek silver coin of the period of Peter the Great was known as a **piaty-altynny**.

Altynnik   3-kopek coin of the Soviet Union since 1926, derived from the **altyn** or 6-**denga** coin of the Middle Ages, *alty* being the Tatar word for six.

Aluminium (American **Aluminum**)   Silvery light-weight metal, chemical symbol *Al*, developed commercially in the late 19th century for commemorative medals, but used for tokens and emergency money during World War I and since 1940 widely used in subsidiary coinage.

Aluminium-Bronze   Alloy of aluminium and copper. Hard-wearing and gold-coloured, it is now widely used in tokens and subsidiary coinage.

Amani   Gold unit of weight in Afghanistan.

Anepigraphic   Denotes coins or medals without a legend.

Angel   Medieval gold coin deriving its name from the effigy of the Archangel Michael. First struck in France in 1341 and known as the *ange d'or*, it was copied in Flanders and Brabant and adopted in English in 1465. The **obverse** showed the monarch standing in a ship while the **reverse** showed Michael battling with a dragon. This gold coin was struck until the outbreak of the Civil War in 1642 and was popular as a **touchpiece**, which explains why so many examples have been pierced for suspension round the neck.

Anna   Unit of currency in India until 1955, worth 12 pies or 4 pice, and 16 annas being worth a rupee. 2-anna pieces were the smallest silver coins under British rule, but annas were struck in bronze (1907–47) or cupro-nickel, followed by similar republican pieces up to 1955.

Annealing   Process of heating and cooling applied to metal to relieve stresses and prepare it for striking into coins and medals.

Annulet   Small circle often used an ornament or spacing device in coin legends.

Antimony   Brittle white metal, chemical symbol Sb (from Latin *stibnum*), virtually impractical as a coinage metal but used for the Chinese 10 cents of Kweichow, 1931. Alloyed with tin, copper or lead, it produces the white metal popular as a medallic medium.

Antoniniani   Silver coins minted in Imperial Rome. The name derives from the Emperor Caracalla (Marcus Aurelius Antoninus) in whose reign they were first struck and tariffed as double-**denarii** (A.D. 214). The silver content was progressively reduced and by the time of the last antoniniani, in A.D. 295, they had been reduced to a **billon** alloy.

Ar.   Abbreviation for Latin *Argentum* (silver), used for coins struck in this metal.

Argentino   Gold coin worth 5 pesos and similar to the British **sovereign** in size, minted by Argentina from 1881 to 1896. The half argentino was worth 2.5 pesos.

As   Shortened form of *As Libra*, the Roman pound, forming the unit of the **Aes grave** currency. The as was divided into the semis (half), triens (third), quadrans (quarter), sextans (sixth) and uncia (ounce or twelfth). By about 130 B.C. the as had become a copper coin (16 asses = 1 **denarius**) and by the mid-3rd century A.D., 4 asses = 1 **sestertius**.

Ashrafi   Gold coin worth a Venetian **zecchino**, issued in Persia 15th–18th centuries, and imitated by Afghanistan and the Indian states of Awadh, Bahawalpur and Hyderabad.

Asper   Silver coin of the secessionary Trebizond empire (1204–1461), portraying the emperor (obverse) and St. Eugenius (reverse).

Assay mark   Mark applied to a medal struck in precious metal by an assayer or assay office as a guarantee of the fineness of the metal.

Assignat   Type of paper money issued in France, 1789–96, representing land assigned to the holders. Assignats were devised as a temporary measure to overcome the shortage of metallic currency and were originally mortgage bonds on the lands confiscated from the Church. They were interest-bearing and legal tender, but over-issue led to their depreciation to a thirtieth of their face value. They were superseded by the **mandats** which, themselves, rapidly depreciated.

At   Subsidiary coin in Laos; 100 at = 1 **kip**.

Att   Small copper coin of Thailand, struck till 1882; 64 att = 1 **tical** or **baht**.

Au.   Abbreviation of the Latin *Aurum* (gold), denoting coins in this metal.

August d'or   Gold coin worth 5 **talers**, struck on behalf of Frederick Augustus III of Saxony in the late 18th century. Half and double augusts were also minted.

Augustale   Handsome gold coin first struck in 1231 by the Emperor Frederick II as King of Sicily at Messina and Brindisi. It took its name from the portrayal of the Hohenstauffen ruler after the manner of Augustus Caesar. The augustale was worth 7.5 **tari** and there was also a comparatively rare half augustale.

Aurar   Plural form of **eyrir**, the smallest unit of currency used in Iceland, the 100th part of the **kronur**.

Aureus (Latin for golden)   The term for the Roman unit of gold coinage was *nummus aureus* (literally gold coin) but it was soon shortened to *aureus*. Originally tariffed at 25 silver **denarii**, or 40 to the Roman pound of gold, it fluctuated in weight and value and by the time of Diocletian in the late 3rd century had been reduced to 70 to the pound. Its half was the **quinarius** and its double the **binio**.

Aurichalcum   Latinised from the Greek term *orichalcos*, it signifies "gold bronze" and denotes an alloy of copper and zinc to form brass, used in Imperial Rome for **dupondii**, semisses and **sestertii**.

Autodollar   Name given to the silver **yüan** issued in the Chinese province of Kweichow in 1928 and having a contemporary motor car as the obverse motif.

Auxiliary Payment Certificate   Form of paper money intended for use by American military personnel stationed in overseas countries. Periodically these certificates would be replaced by entirely new issues, all personnel being confined to camp while the changeover was made, so that civilians who had amassed vast quantities of these notes illegally would be unable to get rid of the obsolete notes.
See also **baf** and **scrip**.

Avo   Subsidiary coin used in the Portuguese colony of Macau; 100 avo = 1 **pataca**.

B

Babel Note   Nickname given to the paper money of the Russian Socialist Federated Soviet Republic (1919) because it bore the slogan "workers of the world unite" in seven languages, a reference to the biblical tower of Babel.

Baf   Acronym from British Armed Forces – the popular name for the vouchers which could only be exchanged for goods in service canteens. First issued in 1945, they were subsequently provided in many post-war campaigns as well as in British garrisons and bases all over the world in time of peace.

Bagarone   Popular name for the half **bolognino**, minted in Bologna and other Italian cities in the 15th century.

Bagattino   Small Venetian copper coin, worth a sixth of a **grosso**, minted between 1423 and 1573.

Bäggliangster   Small copper coin issued by Lucerne in the 16th–17th centuries, portraying St. Leodegar, the cantonal patron saint. The name is derived from a fancied resemblance of the chubby saint to a kind of bun (*bäggli*).

Baht   Thai unit of currency, divided into 100 **atts** or **satangs**.

Baiocco (plural Baiocchi)   The smallest silver coin issued by the Papal States, introduced in 1464 as a successor to the **bolognino**. It was debased to **billon** in the 16th century and to copper in 1726. 1 baiocco = 5 **quattrini** and in the reign of Pius IX copper coins worth 2 and 5 baiocchi were also struck.

Banica   Unit of currency in Croatia, 1941–5. 100 banicas = 1 **kuna**.

Banknote   Paper money issued by a bank and usually promising to pay the bearer on demand in coin of the realm. Banknotes had their origins in the **promissory notes** of the medieval bankers or the receipts given by goldsmiths for valuables deposited with them for safe-keeping. The first printed banknotes were issued by the Stockholm Bank in 1661–6, and were followed by the issues of the Bank of England (1695), the Bank of Scotland (1696) and the French Banque Générale (1716). The use of banknotes was greatly extended from 1914 onwards, following the suspension of **specie** payments and the gradual decline in the use of precious metal coinage.

Bank tokens   Silver pieces issued by the Bank of England (1804 and 1811–16) and the Bank of Ireland (1804–13) to meet the shortage of silver coinage issued by the government. The Bank of England authorised five-shilling pieces, with an inscription countermarked by Boulton of the Soho Mint, Birmingham on contemporary Spanish dollars, while the later Bank of England tokens comprised 18 pence and 3-shilling silver tokens (a similar piece valued at 9 pence was an **essay**). The Bank of Ireland tokens consisted of 5, 10 and 30 pence and 6 shilling tokens.

Banu (plural **Bani**)   Subsidiary unit in the coinage of Romania. 100 bani = 1 **leu**. The decimal system was introduced in 1867 when Romania join the **Latin Monetary Union** and subsequently issued bronze coins in denominations of 1, 2, 5, 10 and 50 bani. Cupro-nickel, aluminium, brass, aluminium-bronze and nickel-steel used for bani since 1900 indicate the economic fluctuations of Romania.

Bar   Metal **clasp** mounted on a medal ribbon to denote a second award of a decoration, but also loosely applied to campaign clasps.

Barbarina   Silver coin worth 10 **soldi**, issued by Mantua in the 16th–17th centuries.

Barbarous copies   Coins modelled on classical originals, issued by the Celtic and Germanic tribes beyond the frontiers of the Roman Empire. Greek **staters** and Roman **denarii** were the coins most frequently copied but they can easily be distinguished by their crude parodies of the original portraiture and the blundered inscriptions.

Barbone   Silver coin worth 12 soldi, issued by the Italian republic of Lucca in the 15th–18th centuries. The name was derived from the bearded portrait of Christ on the obverse. A similar coin tariffed at **6 soldi** was the **barbonaccio** (or little barbone).

Barbuda   Portuguese for "bearded" and the name given to a billon coin worth 3 dinheiros struck in the reign of Ferdinand I (1367–83).

Bar cent   Unofficial cent of English origin, produced as a prototype for the United States coinage in 1785, with the monogram USA (obverse) and 13 horizontal bars (reverse). The design is supposed to have been copied from an old American Continental Army button.

Bath metal   Inferior bronze alloy (copper 97.6, tin 2.2, iron .04, zinc trace), named after the English city where it was used for casting cannon. It was used by William Wood of Bristol for Irish and American tokens (**Wood's Halfpence**) and also by Amos Topping for Manx coins, 1733–4.

Batzen   Silver coin popular in southern Germany, Bohemia and Switzerland from the late 15th century. The first batzen, worth 4 **kreuzers**, were issued by Berne in 1492 and the name is said to be derived from the local word for bear, alluding to the motif on the city's coat of arms. Batzen continued in Switzerland till 1850 when the coinage was decimalised, and even thereafter the term has survived colloquially to denote the 10-**rappen** coin.

Bawbee   Three derivations are given for this once common Scottish coin. The least likely is from *bas billon* (French for billon of poor quality), and the most plausible is from the Scottish word for "baby" – a reference to its diminutive value. The most original explanation derives it from Alexander Orrok, Laird of Sillebawbee, Master of the Mint in the reign of James V (1513–42) in which the coin was first minted. Worth sixpence Scots or one English halfpenny, the bawbee has survived in local parlance as a synonym for a halfpenny.

Bazarucco   Subsidiary coin of Goa and Diu introduced by the Portuguese in 1510 and variously tariffed from 2 to 20 **reis**. It was struck in copper and latterly tin, and survived till the early 19th century.

Beading   Ornamental border found on the raised rim of a coin.

Behelfszahlungsmittel   German term for auxiliary payment certificates in denominations of **pfennigs** and **marks** used in occupied Europe from 1939 to 1945. These notes were issued to German troops at a value ten times greater than that printed on them, but when civilians came to redeem them they received only nominal value for them.

Belga   Term adopted by Belgium in 1926 as money of account (5 **francs** = 1 belga), though the word appeared, with its equivalent in francs, on some of the high denomination coins of the 1930s.

Bell metal   Alloy of copper and tin normally used in the casting of bells, but employed for the subsidiary coinage of the French Revolutionary period.

Besa, Beza   see **Paisa**

Bezant   Medieval gold coin, widely used in Europe and originating in Constantinople. The name was derived from Byzantium. Apart from the Byzantine coins of the 4th–15th centuries, bezants were minted by the Saracens and the Crusader kingdoms of Cyprus and Jerusalem.

Bianco (plural **bianchi**)   Italian word for white, denoting a silver coin worth 10 **bolognini** or half a **lira** minted by Bologna and the Papacy, 16th–18th centuries.

Bill of exchange   An unconditional order in writing, addressed by one person to another, signed by the person giving it, requiring the person to whom it is addressed to pay on demand or at a fixed or determinable future time, a certain sum in money to or to the order of a specified person or bearer. The earliest bills were entirely handwritten but from 1800 onwards printed elements appear, and they reached their peak in the mid-19th century when pictorial vignettes and ornament were in vogue. These printed bills were the forerunners of the special cheques used by businesses today.

Billon   Silver alloy containing less than 50% fine silver, usually mixed with copper. Billon was widely used in classical times, from Armorica to the Aegean, usually in times of economic crises, and was also utilised in European subsidiary coinage in the 17th–19th centuries. In Spain this alloy was known as *vellon*.

Bimetallism   Monetary system in which two metals are in simultaneous use and equally available as legal tender, imply-ing a definite ratio in value between the two. A double stan-dard of gold and silver, with a ratio around 16 : 1, existed till the mid-19th century when international economics began to favour a single gold standard, even though coins of other metals (silver, cupro-nickel, copper, etc.) continued as sub-sidiary or token coinage.

Binio   Name given to the gold double aureus of Imperial Rome, minted in the reigns of Caracalla, Julia Domna and Elagabalus.

Birr   Unit of currency in Ethiopia since 1976. 100 cents = 1 birr.

Birthday coins   Coins issued to celebrate the birthday of a ruler or member of the ruling family originated in Imperial Rome, notably the reigns of Maximianus (286–305) and Constantinus I (307–37). Silver **talers** celebrating the ruler's birthday were issued by several German states, and in more recent times the most notable examples have included the series issued by Bavaria to mark the 90th birthday of Prince Regent Luitpold, the Swedish coins celebrating the 70th, 80th and 90th birthdays of Gustav Adolf VI, and recent coins of the British Commonwealth honouring the Queen Mother, the Prince of Wales and the Duke of Edinburgh.

Bit   Term denoting fragments of large silver coins, cut up and circulating as fractional values. Spanish dollars or 8-**real**

pieces were frequently broken up for circulation in the American colonies and the West Indies. Though long bits and short bits circulated at 15 and 10 cents respectively, the term gradually came to be equated with the real (12½ ¢), hence the American colloquialism – "two-bit" signifying a quarter (dollar). The term became the unit of currency in the Danish West Indies, 1904–17, 500 bits = 100 **cents** = 5 **francs** = 1 **daler**.

Black Farthing Nickname given to the copper **farthing** struck in the reign of James III of Scotland (1460–88), the first copper coin of the British Isles since Roman times. The term is also applied loosely to farthings issued from 1897 onwards with a black finish to distinguish them from the gold half **sovereigns** of similar size.

Black Money English term for the debased silver **deniers** minted in France which circulated widely in England until they were banned by government decree in 1351.

Blaffert (**Plappart**) Base silver coin worth 3 **kreuzers**, circulating in 15th century Switzerland, and believed to have been the earliest coin to bear Arabic numerals and a date in the Christian era.

Blank Piece of metal, cut or punched out of a rolled bar or strip, and prepared for striking to produce coins or medals. Alternative terms are **flan** and **planchet**.

Blauwe Gulden Dutch term signifying "blue guilder", used to denote the 15th–16th century **goldgulden** struck from greatly debased silver.

Blob Popular name for the copper 5-cent piece issued by Ceylon in 1909–10.

Blood Klippe (Swedish **blodsklipping**) Silver pieces struck at Vadstena in 1568 by the brothers Johan, Duke of Finland, and Karl, Duke of Södermanland, to pay their troops during their campaign against their brother Eric XIV. The name is an allusion to the fact that the silver came from the treasure which Eric had seized after the murder of Svante Sture in Uppsala (1567).

Blundered inscription   Legend in which the lettering is jumbled or meaningless, indicating the illiteracy of the barbarous tribes who copied Greek and Roman coins, or the medieval moneyers responsible for coining silver pennies in some provincial mints.

Bodle (otherwise known as a **turner**)   Small Scottish copper coin valued at 2d Scots or a sixth of an English penny, minted between 1604 and 1697. The nickname "bodle" seems to have first been used about 1642, but it is doubtful whether it derived from the name Bothwell as some etymologists have suggested.

Bogash (**bogach, bogache**)   Copper coin of the Yemen. 40 bogash = 20 **piastres** = 1 **imadi** or **ryal**.

Bolivar   Unit of currency in Venezuela (= 100 **centimos**), named after Simon Bolivar (1783–1830,) leader of the struggle of the Spanish American colonies for independence from the mother country.

Boliviano   Unit of currency in Bolivia (= 100 **centavos**).

Bolognino   Silver coins minted by the Italian city-state of Bologna from 1191 onwards. By 1236 one bolognino grosso was tariffed at 12 bolognini piccoli. Bolognini were subsequently struck in Aquila and Modena.

Bonk   Emergency money consisting of pieces cut from copper bars, used in Dutch colonies. Bonks worth 4.75 **stuivers** were issued in Ceylon in 1785, and in various values from half to 8 stuivers in the Dutch East Indies, from 1800 to 1818.

Bonnet Piece   Scottish gold coin, minted in 1539–40 from gold mined at Leadhills. The name is derived from the obverse portraying King James V in a large flat bonnet.

Bon Pour   French for "good for", inscribed on Chamber of Commerce tokens issued in 1923 during a shortage of legal tender coinage.

Botdrager (Dutch for "pot-bearer")   Nickname given to a doppelgroschen first minted by Louis le Male for

Flanders in 1365. It derives its sobriquet from the obverse motif showing a lion upholding a helmet resembling the cooking pots of the period.

Bouquet Sou   Canadian copper token halfpenny of 1837, deriving its name from the nosegay of heraldic flowers on the obverse.

Box coin   Small container formed by obverse and reverse of two coins, hollowed out and screwed together.

Box medal   Medal deliberately manufactured in two parts that unscrew to reveal a cavity usually containing card or paper discs bearing engravings of a commemorative nature.

Bracteate   (**Latin** *bractea* meaning thin piece of metal)   Coins struck on blanks so thin that the image applied to one side appears in reverse on the other. First minted in Erfurt and Thuringia in the 12th century, bracteates were also produced in Hesse, Brandenburg, Swabia, Switzerland, Bohemia, Silesia, Scandinavia and Poland up to the early 14th century.

Brasher Doubloon   Unofficial gold coin of 408 grains produced as a pattern for American coinage by the jeweller Ephraim Brasher of New York, 1787.

Braspenning   Dutch silver coin worth 2-**groot** (later 2.5-groot) or 1.25-**stuiver**, first struck in Flanders in 1409.

Brass   Alloy of copper and zinc, widely used for subsidiary coinage in this century. The term was also used formerly for the alloy of copper and tin now known as bronze, and occurs numismatically in the designation of Roman subsidiary coinage as first, second or third brass.
See also **tombac**.

Breeches money   Derisive term given by the Royalists to the coinage of the Commonwealth, 1651, the conjoined elongated oval shields on the reverse resembling a pair of breeches.

Brick tea money   Slabs of compressed tea leaves, bearing Chinese characters signifying weight and quality, were used as currency by the nomads of Central Asia, particularly in Turkestan, Szechwan and Tibet, during the first half of the 20th century.

Broad   Gold coin of 20 **shillings** introduced in England during the Commonwealth period and retained in the early years of the reign of Charles II.

Brockage   Mis-struck coin with only one design, normal on one side and **incuse** on the other. This occurs when a coin previously struck adheres to the die and strikes the next blank to pass through the press.

Bronze   Alloy of copper and tin, first used as a coinage metal by the Chinese *c*. 1000 B.C. and in the western world by the Greeks in the late 5th century B.C. Often used synonymously with copper, though it should be noted that bronze only superseded copper as the constituent of the base metal British coins in 1860.

Bu (boo) see **Pu**

Bungtown coppers (from Anglo-American slang *bung*, to swindle or bribe)   Derisory term for halfpence of English or Irish origin, often counterfeit, which circulated in North American towards the end of the colonial period.

Butut   Subsidiary coinage of The Gambia, introduced in 1971. 100 bututs = 1 **dalasi**.

C

Cabinet piece   Term denoting a coin or medal in the very finest condition, an allusion to the specimens which were considered worthy of inclusion in the cabinets of the Renaissance princes who revived the fashion for coin collecting, dormant since Roman Imperial times.

Calderilla   Spanish copper coin worth 8 **maravedis**, struck by authority of Philip IV from 1635 to 1654. Later examples were countermarked and retariffed at 12 **maravedis**.

Candareen (candarin)   Chinese unit of weight (100 candareen = 10 **mace** = 1 **tael**). Silver coins issued by the provinces during the Manchu Empire bore values expressed in dollars or cents, with their equivalents in **mace** and candareens. Thus the silver **yüan** or dollar was inscribed "7 mace and 2 candareens" and the 50 cents "3 mace and 6 candareens".

Cannon money   Cast bronze cannon used as currency in Sabah (North Borneo). These pieces were modelled on Portuguese ships' cannons and were frequently decorated with figures of dogs, pigs, crocodiles or tigers. They ranged between 20 and 35 cm in length and weighed up to 2.5 kg. Though they died out early this century their memory is perpetuated on the reverse of the Brunei dollar introduced in 1970.

Carat   Originally a unit of weight for precious stones, based on leguminous seeds (*ceratia*), it is also used to denote the fineness or purity of precious metals, being 1/24th part of the whole. Thus 9 carat gold is .375 fine and 22 carat, the English **sovereign** standard, is .916 fine.

Carlin   Name given to coins issued by authority of Charles of Anjou in 1278 for the Kingdom of Sicily and struck in gold (*carlin d'or*) or silver (*carlin d'argent*). Gold and silver carlins formed the basis of Sicilian coinage till the unification of Italy in 1860.

Carlino   Variant of the above adopted by Pope Martin V in 1430 for the Papal States. At various times it was tariffed at 7.5 or 10 **baiocchi**, while the doppio carlino of the 18th century was worth 15 baiocchi.

Cartwheel   Popular term for the large and cumbersome penny and twopenny pieces of 1797 weighing one and two ounces, struck by Matthew Boulton at the Soho Mint, Birmingham. The cartwheels were the first regular issue of copper pence in Britain and followed a period in which the public had had to rely on token coppers.

Cased set   Sets of coins in mint condition, housed in the official cases issued by the mint. Formerly blue plush or velvet lining was used, but nowadays many sets are encapsulated in plastic to facilitate handling.

Cash (from Portuguese *caixa*, Hindi *kasu*)   Round piece of bronze or brass with a square hole in the centre, used as subsidiary coinage in China for almost 2000 years till the early 20th century. In Chinese these pieces were known as *Ch'ien* or *Li* and strung together in groups of 1000 were equivalent to a silver **tael**.

Cast coins   Coins cast from molten metals in moulds. This technique, widespread in the case of early commemorative medals and communion tokens, has been used infrequently in coins, the vast majority of which are die-struck. Examples of cast coins include the Chinese cash and the Manx halfpenny and penny of 1709.

Cauri   Unit of currency in Guinea since 1971 (100 = 1 syli), derived from the **cowrie** depicted on the 50 ¢ coin.

Cedi   Unit of currency in Ghana, adopted in 1965, and divided into 100 **pesewas**.

Ceitil The earliest copper coin issued in Europe since Roman times, it was first issued in Portugal in the reign of Alfonso III (1248–79) and on a regular basis from 1415 onwards. The ceitil was worth a sixth of a **real**.

Cent Derived from the Latin *centum* = hundredth, it was introduced by the United States in 1792 and has since served as a model for many other decimal systems. It was adopted by the Netherlands in 1816, and subsequently by Liberia (1833), Canada (1858), Ceylon (1870), Mauritius (1877), East Africa (1906), British West Indies (1952), South Africa (1961), Australia (1966) and New Zealand (1967) among others, now totalling over fifty countries.

Centas (plural forms **centu, centai**) Unit of currency in Lithuania, 1925–40; 100 centai = 1 **litas**.

Centavo Unit of currency in Portugal and its overseas territories, as well as the Philippines and many countries of Latin America.

Centenionalis Bronze coin introduced as part of the currency reforms effected by the joint emperors Constans and Constantius II in A.D. 337. The centenionalis and its half were struck till A.D. 360.

Centesimo Unit of currency adopted in Sardinia in 1823 and extended to the unified Italy in 1861 (100 centesimi = 1 **lira**). Centesimi subsequently spread to Chile, the Dominican Republic, Panama, Paraguay and Uruguay as well as the Italian colonies and associated states (San Marino and the Vatican).

Centime Unit of currency adopted by Revolutionary France in 1793 (100 centimes = 1 **franc**), and since extended to the countries of the French Community, as well as Belgium, Luxembourg and Switzerland.

Centimo Unit of currency in Spain (100 centimos = 1 **peseta**), introduced in 1864 and later used at various times by Costa Rica, Paraguay, Peru, the Philippines and Venezuela.

Chaise d'or French for "gold throne", an allusion to the obverse motif showing the enthroned monarch. First minted in 1303 under Philippe IV of France, it was copied by Ludwig of Bavaria (1314–47) at the Antwerp mint and served as the model for the gold **florin** struck by Edward III of England in 1344.

Cheque or **Check**   A bill of exchange drawn on a banker, payable on demand. They differ essentially from the earlier **bills of exchange** in that they are invariably drawn on a bank and never a person or firm. Entirely handwritten cheques are known from about 1660 but by 1790 printed cheque forms were coming into use. From 1810 cheques became much more formal in appearance and greater attention was paid to fine engraving, reaching its height between 1840 and 1900.

See also **Special Cheque**.

Chervonetz   Russian word for **ducat** and popularly applied to the Hungarian and Dutch gold coins that circulated in Russia in imperial times. In 1923 the Bolshevik regime struck 10-**rouble** gold pieces known by this name, mainly as a propaganda exercise as none ever circulated in the Soviet Union. The chervonetz was revived for a limited issue in the same design in 1975.

Chetrum   Unit of currency in Bhutan, 100 chetrums = 1 **ngultrum** or **rupee**. Subsidiary coinage in chetrums has been issued since 1974.

Cheun   Unit of currency in South Korea, 100 = 1 **won**.

Chiao   Unit of currency in China and Taiwan, worth 10 cents (**fen**) or a tenth of a dollar (**yüan**).

Cho-gin   Silver ingots used as currency in Japan during the Shogunate (1582–1868).

Chon   Unit of currency in North Korea (100 = 1 **won**). Aluminium 1, 5 and 10 chon coins were introduced in 1959.

Chop-marks (from Hindi *chop* = seal)   Counter-marks, usually consisting of a single character, applied by Chinese merchants to precious metal coins and ingots as a guarantee of their weight and fineness. Coins may be found with a wide variety of chop-marks and the presence of several different marks on the same coin considerably enhances its interest and value.

Chuckram Unit of currency in the Indian princely state of Travancore until 1945, 1 and 2 chuckram coins being struck in copper and silver respectively. 4 chuckrams = 1 **fanam**.

Cistophori Greek for "chest-bearing", a generic term for the coins of Pergamum with an obverse motif of a chest showing a serpent crawling out of the half-opened lid. Cistophori became very popular all over Asia Minor in the 3rd–2nd centuries B.C. and were struck also at mints in Ionia, Phrygia, Lydia and Mysia.

Clad coins see **Sandwich**

Clash marks Mirror image traces found on a coin which has been struck from a pair of dies, themselves damaged by having been struck together without a blank between.

Clasp Bar worn on the ribbon of campaign medals, denoting battles and campaigns for which the medal was awarded.

Clipped coins Precious metal coins from which small amounts have been removed by clipping the edges. It was to prevent this that graining and edge inscriptions were adopted.

Cob Crude, irregularly shaped silver piece, often with little more than a vestige of die impressions, produced in the Spanish American mints in the 16th–18th centuries.

Coin Piece of metal, marked with a device, issued by government authority and intended for use as money.

Coin note Note issued by the United States Treasury, back by silver bullion set aside for the purpose. Anyone presenting one of these notes for redemption has to be paid in silver dollars, though such is their rarity that they are worth much more than their equivalent in silver.

Colon Unit of currency in Costa Rica (= 100 **centimos**) and El Salvador (= 100 **centavos**), from the Spanish version of Columbus.

Commemorative Coin, medal, token or paper note issued to celebrate a current event or the anniversary of a historic event or personality. Such items are often restricted in circulation, or struck in precious metal as collector's pieces rather than for general circulation. Good examples include the American half dollars, 1893–1954, and British crowns since 1935. Many of the Roman "large brass" were commemorative in purpose, as were the numerous **talers** of the German principalities and the 5- and 10-**mark** pieces of more recent times. Though dollar- or crown-sized coins are favoured for commemoratives, small denominations have occasionally been used (e.g. Australian **florins**, 1927–54; Canada nickel-industry **nickel**, 1951, and Mounted Police **quarter**, 1973). Double dates have been used by Canada and the United States on a range of circulating coins to indicate commemoration, while the Isle of Man added the Millennium symbol to coins issued in 1979 to celebrate the island's thousandth anniversary of independence. Commemorative paper money is much less common, the best known examples being many of the **Notgeld** issues of Germany, 1918–23. Others include notes issued by Haiti (1904), Mexico (1910, Canada (1935 and 1967), Colombia (1938), Cuba (1953), the Dominican Republic (1955), Venezuela (1967) the United States (1976) and the Isle of Man (1979).

Communion tokens   Tickets distributed to those who had passed catechismal examination and were therefore fit to partake of Communion according to the Calvinist and Presbyterian rites. John Calvin is credited with their invention in 1561, but they are referred to in the minutes of the first Scottish General Assembly in 1560. Later they were adopted by most of the Reformed churches and were widespread in Switzerland, Huguenot France, Germany, the Low Countries, Scandinavia, Scotland and Scottish settlements overseas. The earliest types were cast in lead, but later they were struck in pewter, brass, bronze or white metal, with the name of the parish, the date, the minister's name or initials, occasionally (in larger congregations) the number of the sitting, and even pictorial elements. Most 19th century examples include biblical quotations. Metal tokens have gradually given way to card tickets since the beginning of this century, but survive in North America, mainly as commemoratives.

Compound Interest Notes   Notes issued by the United States Treasury, 1863–4 during the Civil War when the Federal government was facing bankruptcy. These notes, in denominations from $10 to $1,000, earned interest at 6%, compounded twice a year for a period of three years.

Condition   The state of a coin or medal, according to the freshness of its appearance, or the degree of wear evident. The six main collectable grades of condition are given below, with their equivalents in other languages, internationally recognised by dealers and auctioneers.

English	French	German	Italian	Spanish
Proof	Flan bruni	Polierte Platte	Fondo specchio	Placa pulimentada
Brilliant uncirculated (BU)	Fleur de Coin (FDC)	Stempelglanz	Fior di conio	Flor de cuño
Extremely fine (EF)	Superbe (SU)	Vorzüglich	Splendido	Extraordinariamente bien conservado
Very fine (VF)	Très beau (TB)	Sehr schön	Bellissimo	Muy bien conservado
Fine (F)	Beau	Schön	Molto bello	Bien conservado
Very good (VG)	Très bien conservé	Sehr gut erhalten	Bello	Regular conservacion

Conjoined   Term denoting overlapped profiles of two or more rulers (e.g. William and Mary).

Contorniate (from Italian *contorno* = edge)   Late 4th–5th century Roman bronze piece whose name alludes to the characteristic grooving on the edges. Many examples depict circus activities and it is thought that they served either as tickets of admission or prize money in circuses.

Contribution coin   Name given to coins, mainly convention **talers** and **ducats**, struck by Bamberg, Eichstatt, Fulda, Mainz, Trier and Würzburg in the 1790s during the First Coalition War against the French Republic. The name alludes to the fact that the bullion used to produce the coins necessary to pay troops was raised by contribution from the Church and the civilian population.

Convention Money   Any system of coinage agreed by neighbouring countries for mutual acceptance and interchange. Examples include the amphictyonic coins of Ancient Greece, the Austrian and Bavarian **talers** and **gulden** (1753–1857) which were copied by other south German states and paved the way for the German Monetary Union.

Copper   Metallic element, chemical symbol Cu, widely used as a coinage metal for 2,500 years. Pure or almost pure copper was used for subsidiary coinage in many countries till the mid-19th century, but has since been superseded by copper alloys which are cheaper and more hard-wearing: **bronze** (copper and tin), **brass** (copper and zinc), **Bath metal** or **bell metal** (low-grade copper and tin), **aluminium-bronze** (copper and aluminium), pewter (tin and lead with a little copper), potin (copper, tin, lead and silver), **German silver** (copper, zinc and nickel) or **cupro-nickel** (cooper and nickel). Copper is also alloyed with gold and silver, and when the copper content exceeds the silver content the alloy is known as **billon**.

Copperhead   Nickname given to token cents issued by tradesmen, institutions and even private individuals to alleviate the shortage of government coinage during the American Civil War. They first appeared in Cincinnati in 1862 and over 5,000 different types were issued before they were suppressed at the end of 1863.

Coppernose   Popular name for the debased silver **shillings** of Henry VIII. Many of them were struck in copper with little more than a silver wash which tended to wear off at the highest point of the obverse, the nose on the full-face portrait of the king.

Cordoba   Unit of currency in Nicaragua (= 100 **centavos**).

Cornuto   Silver coin issued by authority of Charles II of Savoy, 1543 and worth 5 **grossi**.

Corôa de prata   Portuguese silver crown-sized coin worth 1000 **reis**, issued in 1836–45.

Corona   Neapolitan silver coin introduced by Robert of Anjou (1309–43) and deriving its name from the crown depicted on the obverse.

Coronato   Originally a **billon** coin minted under Sancho IV of Castile (1284–95), but also a silver **grosso** struck to commemorate the coronation of Ferdinand I of Naples (1458–94).

Corrosion   Rusting and pitting of the surface of a coin, caused by chemical action e.g. atmospheric pollution, salts in the ground where coins have been buried, sea water, etc.

Counter   Metal disc, often resembling a coin, used in medieval accountancy and a speciality of the minters of Nuremberg. The term is also used to denote pieces used in gambling.

Counterfeit   Imitation of a coin, token or piece of paper money, intended for circulation to deceive the public and defraud the state. Legislation in many countries provides severe penalties for counterfeiting money and inscriptions to this effect will be found on many banknotes. Even the mere possession of counterfeit notes and coins may be a criminal offence. Counterfeit gold or silver coins, struck from inferior alloys, do not ring true when dropped on a hard surface, and can generally be detected by the irregularity in the reeding or graining of the edge.

Countermark   Punch mark applied to a coin some time after its original issue, either to alter its nominal value, or to authorise its circulation in some other country. Examples include the base-silver **shillings** of Edward VI countermarked in 1559 for circulation at a lower value, and the Spanish **dollars** with George III's effigy countermarked in 1804 for circulation as 4s 9d.

Couronne d'or   French gold coin introduced in 1340 in the reign of Philippe VI and deriving its name from the principal motif of a crown.

Cowrie   Small shell (*Cypraea moneta*) circulating as a form of primitive currency from 1000 B.C. (China) to the present century (East and West Africa) and also used in the islands of the Indian and Pacific Oceans. In the late 19th century 200 cowries = 1 Indian **rupee**. It gives its name to the unit of currency (**cauri**) used in Guinea since 1971.

Crossazzo Large silver coin of Genoa, introduced in 1666, deriving its name from the cross and stars motif on the reverse. Double and quadruple crossazzi were also minted.

Crown English coin worth 5 **shillings** (25 new pence). It was introduced in 1526 by Henry VIII as a small gold coin worth 4s 6d (the crown of the rose), but superseded within three months by the crown of the double rose worth 5s. Gold crowns survived as late as 1762 but were only minted sporadically. The familiar large-sized silver crown was introduced by Edward VI in 1551 and the large diameter permitted an equestrian portrait of the ruler, a tradition maintained by the Stuarts and revived for the Coronation and Silver Jubilee crowns of 1953 and 1977. The crown attained its present size in 1816 when the George and Dragon motif by Pistrucci was adopted. Many crowns of George III to Queen Victoria bore a regnal date on the edge, in addition to the calendar year. Since 1900 crowns have not been struck for general circulation, but were included in the specimen sets during coronation years (1902, 1937, 1953). From 1927 to 1936 small quantities were struck about Christmas-time for people to give as presents, and commemorative crowns were issued from 1935 onwards to celebrate jubilees and important events and personalities. Crowns, mainly for commemorative purposes, have also been issued by many British Commonwealth countries and the term "crown" appears as a denomination on commemorative pieces of the Cayman Islands, although no such unit of currency is generally used there, the currency consisting of **dollars** and **cents**.

Cruzadinho Small Portuguese gold coin, authorised by Joao V (1706–50) and worth 400 **reis**. They were struck at the mints in Lisbon, Rio de Janeiro and Minas Gerais in Brazil, and derived their name from the obverse motif of a cross.

Cruzado Originally a gold coin issued in the reign of Alfonso V (1438–81), with a cruciform device on the reverse, it was tariffed at 500 **reis** until the 18th century but thereafter the name was transferred to the 400-reis piece. The *cruzado de prata*, worth 400 reis, was a silver coin introduced in 1643 and issued till 1835 when it was superseded by the **corôa de prata**.

Cruzeiro   Brazilian unit of currency introduced in 1942 (= 100 **centavos**). Following the currency reform of 1967, 1 new cruzeiro = 1000 old cruzeiros, a nickel coin of this value being introduced in 1970.

Cuartillo (**cuartilla, cuartino**)   Diminutive forms of the Spanish word for a quarter, used for the tiny silver quarter-**real** coins struck in Mexico, 1796–1808, and the copper coins of the same value issued by the rebels during the War of Independence.

Cuarto   Quarter-**real** coin introduced by Ferdinand and Isabella in 1497 and continuing mainly as a copper coin till 1855 (= 4 **maravedis**). The half-**peso** issued by Bolivia (1830) was also known by this name.

Cumberland Jack   Popular name for a counter or satirical **medalet** of **sovereign** size, struck unofficially in 1837 in brass. In place of the usual George and Dragon motif on the reverse there appears an equestrian figure with the legend "To Hanover" – a reference to the unpopular Duke of Cumberland, uncle of Queen Victoria, who succeeded to Hanoverian throne since Victoria was debarred by Salic law from inheritance as a female.

Cupellation (Latin *cupella* = a little cup)   Process by which gold and silver were separated from lead and other impurities in their ores. A cupel is a shallow cup of bone-ash or other absorbent material which, when hot, absorbs any molten material which wets its surface. Lead melts and oxidises with impurities into the cupel, whereas gold and silver remain on the cupel. Cupellation is also used in assaying the fineness of these precious metals.

Cupro-nickel   Coinage alloy of 75% copper and 25% nickel, now widely used as a base metal substitute for silver. A small amount of zinc is added to the alloy used in modern Russian coins.

Currency   Coins, tokens, paper notes and other articles intended to pass current in general circulation as money.

Customs Gold Units   Paper notes intended primarily for the payment of customs dues but widely accepted as currency. They were introduced by the Kuomintang government of China in 1930 in a bid to end chronic inflation but like their predecessors they rapidly depreciated and eventually notes worth 250,000 units were issued. The last issues appeared during and after the Second World War and were deliberately back-dated by the authorities to give them greater respectability and acceptability.

Cut money   Currency consisting of coins cut into smaller pieces to provide correspondingly smaller denominations. The cruciform device on many medieval coins assisted the division of silver pennies into **halfpence** and **farthings**. The best example of cut money was provided by the Spanish **dollars** of the 17th–19th centuries, frequently divided into bits which themselves became units of currency in America and the West Indies.

D

Daalder   Dutch form of the German word **taler**. The earliest large-sized Dutch silver coins (early 16th century) were known as **Joachimsdaalders**, after the area in Bohemia (Joachimstal) where much of the silver was mined. From 1566 onwards the term **Rijksdaalder** was used for coins tariffed variously at 30 **stuivers** or 1.5 **gulden**.

Dak   Nepalese copper coin of 1891–1911 worth 2 **paise** or the sixteenth of a **mohar**. Bronze 8 dak coins were issued in 1902.

Dala   Polynesian word for **dollar**, denoting the silver dollar issued by authority of King David Kalakaua of Hawaii, 1883.

Dalasi   Unit of currency in The Gambia, introduced in 1971 (= 100 **bututs**).

Daler   Scandinavian form of **taler**, and used as the unit of currency in Denmark, Norway and Sweden prior to the introduction of the decimal system in the 1870s. The daler was worth 6 **marks** in Denmark and 8 marks in Sweden. See also **Rigsdaler, speciedaler**.

Danegeld   English tax originally levied by Aethelred II as a means of raising the tribute which was the price of the temporary cessation of Danish ravages. This device was introduced in 991 and repeated in 994, 1002, 1007 and 1012. Following the accession of Canute in 1016 the original purpose disappeared but it was periodically levied as a war tax thereafter until 1163, being replaced by other imposts of a similar nature but different name. Vast quantities of silver **pennies** were struck to make these enormous payments. Many of the Carolingian **deniers** of France from 864 onwards were minted for the same purpose. More than 22,000

Anglo-Saxon silver pennies have been discovered in a single Gotland hoard alone, and it has been estimated that some £167,000 in tribute money found its way to Scandinavia in the late 10th century.

Daric   Gold coin of ancient Persia, introduced in the reign of Darius I (521–485 B.C.) after whom it was named. The daric weighed 8.4 grams and circulated widely all over the Middle-East and Mediterranean areas, being tariffed at 20 silver **sigloi**.

Darlehnskassen   German term signifying state loan notes issued during the First World War in an abortive bid to fill the shortage of coinage in circulation. These low-denomination notes failed to meet demand and were super-seded by local issues of small **Notgeld** in 1916.

Dauphin   French word for dolphin, a motif which has given its name to two types of French coin. *Le petit dauphin* was a small **billon** coin issued in the province of Dauphiné in the reign of Charles V (1364–80), while the *dauphin de Viennois* denoted small silver or billon coins of the 17th century, last minted at Grenoble in 1702.

Debasement   The reduction in the precious metal content of the coinage, widely practised since time immemorial by governments for economic reasons. Examples include the change from fine gold (.975 fine) to crown gold (.916 fine) in Elizabethan times, and the change from sterling silver (.925 fine) to .500 fine in 1920. During the present century every country formerly using silver has changed to **clad coins** or a base-metal alloy simulating silver (nickel or cupro-nickel).

Decadrachm (dekadrachm)   Large silver coin worth 10 **drachmae**, mainly struck as prize money for the Demareteian Games in Syracuse and known as **demareteion**. Coins of this denomination were also minted at Agrigentum (Akragas) and during the reign of Alexander the Great, as well as by the Hellenistic kingdom of the Ptolemies in Egypt.

Decanummion (dekanummion)   Byzantine copper coin worth 10 **nummi** or a quarter **follis**, first authorised in the reign of Anastasius (491–518) and last issued in 687.

Decimalisation   The adoption of a system of currency in which the principal unit is subdivided into ten, or more commonly 100 fractions. The Tsarina Helena led the world by instituting the **rouble** of 100 **kopeks** in 1534, but other countries lagged behind. The United States adopted the **dollar** of 100 **cents** in 1792 and Revolutionary France introduced the **franc** of 100 **centimes** the following year. Most European countries embraced a decimal system in the course of the 19th century. Britain toyed with the idea, and got as far as introducing the **florin** (inscribed "one tenth of a pound") in 1849, but did not take decimalisation to its logical conclusion until 1971 when the £p system was completed. This left only Malta and Nigeria as the last non-decimal countries in the world, and they followed suit in 1972 and 1973 with the pound (= cents or 1000 **mils**) and the naira (100 **kobo**) respectively.

Décime   French Revolutionary bronze coin worth 10 **centimes** or a tenth of a **franc**, issued in 1796–1801 and revived during the Hundred Days as a form of emergency money.

Decimo   Coin worth 10 **centavos** issued by Chile, Colombia and Ecuador.

Decobolon (dekobolon)   Money of account in ancient Greece signifying 10 **obols** (1.66 **drachmae**).

Decussis   Bronze coin worth 10 **asses** (*decem asses*) issued in the late 3rd century B.C. under the Roman Republic and forming the heaviest piece in the **Aes Grave** series.

Demand note   Emergency issue of paper money by the Federal government following the outbreak of the American Civil War (1861), so-called because of their inscription "promise to pay . . . on Demand". These notes were the original "greenbacks" on account of their predominant colouring but were unique in that they bore neither the Treasury seal nor the name of the U.S. Treasurer and were hand-signed by a large team of clerks in the Treasury Department. They were superseded in 1862 by **Legal Tender Notes**.

Demareteion   Silver **decadrachm** minted by Syracuse in the 5th century B.C. Following the defeat of Carthage at Himera in northern Sicily in 480 B.C., a ransom of 2,000

talents was paid in silver which Gelon, the ruler of Syracuse, had minted as coins given as prizes at the Demareteian Games, named in honour of his consort, Demarete. These coins portrayed the nymph Arethusa and showed a victorious quadriga (war-chariot).

Demonetise   To withdraw coins or paper money from circulation and declare them invalid.

Demy   Scottish gold coin worth 2s 6d, minted in the 14th–15th centuries.

Denar (from Latin *denarius* = penny)   Medieval silver coin minted at the rate of 240 to the Carolingian pound of silver. Eventually the denar or denaro (plural denari) was minted in many parts of Europe from Italy to Hungary. The Emperor Frederick Barbarossa struck the *denaro imperiale* at Noceto *c*. 1160, twice the weight and value of the existing coin, and this was later copied at Milan and other Lombardic mints. The denaro was largely superseded by the **grosso** in the 13th century, but survived in Hungary till the 15th century.

Denarius   Principal silver coin of the Roman Empire, spanning a period from *c*. 211 B.C. till the late 3rd century A.D. The name is derived from Latin *deni* signifying ten, from the fact that the denarius was tariffed at 10 **asses**.

Denga   Late-medieval silver coin in Russia, the name being thought to derive from the Tatar word for **dirhem**. It eventually passed into the Russian language as the word for money (*den'gi*). The value of this coin varied considerably, from 200 to 260 to the **rouble** between the 14th and 16th centuries, but from 1535 onwards it was worth half a **kopek**. From 1700 onwards it was a copper coin, and coins of half its value (a quarter kopek) were also minted till 1916. The 19th century half kopek was popularly known as a denezhka, a diminutive form.

Denier   French for **denarius**, and the term used for the silver **penny** from the 8th century till the reign of Louis XIV. By the 11th century the *denier parisis* was being minted at the rate of 240 to the Parisian **mark**, followed in the next century by the *denier tournois* tariffed at the rate of 5 to 4 of the previous issue. The latter coin was first minted under Philippe

II Auguste at Touraine in 1205. In 1575 it was struck in copper, along with the double **tournois**, the first base-metal coinage in France. By the time of Louis XIII 12 deniers = 4 **liards** = 1 **sol**.

Denning   Small Danish coin, the name being derived from a diminutive form of the Russian **denga** and first struck in the early 17th century with the name and title of Christian IV in Russian. These coins were intended as a medium for trade between Danish merchants and Russian fur-trappers. Similar coins, known as quasi-dennings or rytterpenninge (rider pennies, from the equestrian figure on the obverse), were also minted by several North German principalities (Schleswig-Holstein, Gottorp, Sonderburg-Plön and Bremen) in the same period.

Deut   Small copper coin circulating in Westphalia and the Rhineland in the 17th century, modelled on the contemporary **duit** of the Low Countries.

Diamante   Silver coin instituted by Borso d'Este (1450–71), duke of Ferrara and deriving its name from the diamond-shaped ornament on the shield on the obverse.

Diamantino   Small silver coin of Ferrara worth half a **diamante** and minted till the early 16th century.

Dicken   German expression meaning "the thick one", applied to silver coins minted in Switzerland and southern Germany and modelled on the thick **testone** of northern Italy. The first dicken was struck at Berne in 1482 and tariffed at a third of a Rhenish **guilder**. They were largely superseded by the **guldengroschen** in the mid-16th century.

Didrachm   Small silver coin worth 2 **drachmae**, issued by many of the Greek states in classical times.

Die   Hardened piece of metal bearing a mirror image of the device to be struck on one side of a coin or medal.

Dime   Small silver or (since 1965) cupro-nickel coin worth 10 **cents** or a tenth of a **dollar**. Essays are known from 1792, but were not regularly issued till 1796, but silver half-dimes were minted from 1794 till 1873.

Dinar (plural **dinara**)   Name derived from the **denarius** of the Roman Empire and signifying either a gold coin struck by the Arab caliphates on the model of the Byzantine **solidus**, or a silver coin adopted by Serbia in 1875(=40 **paras**). Both types of dinar survive to this day, the Arab version being the unit of currency in Afghanistan, Algeria, Bahrain, Kuwait, Morocco, Saudi Arabia and Tunisia, while the Serbian version is still the basis of the Yugoslav currency, retariffed at 100 paras.

Diner   Catalan version of **denarius**, inscribed on silver **pseudo-coins** of Andorra since 1960.

Dinero   Spanish version of **denarius** and the name given to the silver **penny** struck under Ferdinand III (1230–53), but debased under his successor Alfonso X, hence the name *dinero negro* (black penny). The same name was used by Peru for the silver coin of 1864–1916 worth a tenth of a **sol**. A half-dinero denomination was minted between 1863 and 1917.

Diobol   Small Greek silver coin worth two **obols** or a third of a **drachma**. Diobols for local currency were struck as copper coins in the Greek areas of the Roman Empire.

Dirhem (**direm**)   Unit of currency in the Arab monetary system, derived from the **drachmae** struck by the Sassanids in Persia. The Ummayad caliphs at first merely added a short Kufic inscription in the wide border of Sassanid drachmae, but Abd al-Malik instituted the silver dirhem in 696 and this circulated widely as a trade coin all over the medieval world. Copper dirhems were also struck by the Near Eastern principalities, and at the present day bronze or cupro-nickel dirhems are used in Iraq, Morocco, Qatar and Dubai.

Disme   Original form of the word **dime**, and as such, inscribed on **patterns** for American 10-cent coins, known as silver or copper, 1792.

Dobla   Spanish word for double, and thus a name applied to several gold coins such as the double **ducat** of Naples and Sicily, and the double **scudo** of Genoa (both 16th century). In Spain it appeared as an adjective in the *dobla castellana* (= 40 maravedis) of Alfonso XI (1313–50) and his successors. The *dobla de la banda*, minted under John II of Castile (1406–54), takes its name from the insignia of the order of chivalry depicted on it.

Doblado   Gold coin worth 2 **escudos** circulating in the Spanish American colonies prior to the War of Independence (1810).

Doblenca (Doblenga)   Small coin worth 2 **deniers**, minted by the Counts of Barcelona in the 12th century and subsequently by the kings of Aragon.

Dobler   Billon coin worth 2 **grossi** struck by the Spanish rulers for circulation in Mallorca from the 14th century onwards. In the late 17th and 18th centuries the coin was struck in copper and reduced in value to 2 **dineros.**

Doblon (doblone, doubloon)   Terms widely used for various coins in Spain and Italy. The *doblon sencillo* was a counter nominally worth 60 **reales**, used in medieval Spanish accountancy, while the only piece actually inscribed *Doblone* was a bronze pattern of Pope Clement XI (1700–21). As a variant of the **dobla**, the doblon or doubloon was the popular name for a succession of Spanish gold coins, from the double **escudo** or **excelente** of the 15th century onwards, the name alluding to the double facing portraits of Ferdinand and Isabella as well as the double value, and this name has survived in Chile and Uruguay to this century for the 10-**peso** gold pieces.

Dodecadrachm   The largest silver coin minted in classical times, struck at Carthage from 237 B.C., following the influx of silver from Iberia resulting from the Carthaginian conquest. It was worth 12 **drachmae.**

Dodecagonal   Twelve-sided, a term applied to the nickel-brass **threepence** of Great Britain, 1937–67.

Doit Alternative spelling of **duit.**

Dokdo   Small copper coin circulating in the Indian states of Junagadh, Kutch and Nawanagar till 1947. 24 dokdo = 1 **kori.**

Dollar   English language equivalent of the German word **taler** and first used to describe the large silver coins of German origin. Later the term was applied in Britain as a nickname for the silver **crown**, though officially the term has only been applied to the 4-**merk** piece of Scotland (1676–82), the Bank of England emergency silver issues, restruck on Spanish 8-**real** pieces (1804) and the large silver trade pieces of 1895–1935. In the American colonies the term was used for the Spanish 8-real piece and this served as the basis for the American decimal system adopted in 1792 (= 100 **cents**). Silver dollars were struck from 1794 to 1803 for general circulation, those dated 1804–39 being rare **patterns** or **essays** only. Circulating dollars were revived in 1840 and, apart from breaks in 1874–7 and 1905–20 continued in silver until 1935. Dollars in the traditional size but cupro-nickel or silver clad, were re-introduced in 1971 with the profile of Eisenhower. In 1979 a much smaller coin intended for general circulation, and portraying Susan B. Anthony, was introduced. American trade dollars were also issued from 1873 to 1885 and gold dollars from 1849 to 1889. The dollar is the principal unit in the decimal system of many countries, from Australia to Trinidad.

Dong   Annamese name for the Chinese **cash** circulating in Indo-China from the 10th century. Originally in bronze, it was re-issued in the 14th century in a tin alloy but by the 19th century had changed to an alloy of copper, tin and zinc, 60 dong being worth 1 **tien** or **tael**. Since 1946 it has been the unit of currency in Vietnam (= 100 **xu**).

Doppia   Italian word for double, applied originally to a gold coin minted in Milan under Galeazzo Maria Sforza (1466–76) and later copied by other cities, such as Bologna, Mantua, Naples and Rome. From 1730 it was the unit of currency in Sardinia, coins being minted from a quarter to 5 doppia. The *doppia domana* was a gold coin worth 30 **paoli**, minted in the Papal States (1776).

Doppietta   Variation of the **doppia**, struck in Turin under Charles Emmanuel III of Savoy for circulation in Sardinia, 1768–72.

Double   Copper coin of Guernsey, derived from the French double **tournois** and minted for general circulation from 1830 till 1938. Higher denominations of 2 to 8 doubles (= 1 **penny**) were minted till 1966.

Douzain   French word for dozen, applied to the **sol tournois** worth 12 **deniers**, first minted under Francis I (1515–47).

Dozzina   Billon coin worth 12 **deniers** minted during the period of papal rule at Avignon.

Drachma   Unit of currency in Greece for 3000 years, derived from the verb *drassomai* = I grasp and originally signifying a handful. This alludes to its meaning in the primitive currency that preceded coinage – a handful of iron rods or spits (*obeliskoi*). When reduced to coinage the silver drachma was reckoned to be worth six copper **obols**. One hundred drachmae were worth 1 **mina** and 6,000 drachmae were worth a **talent** of gold. The drachma and its multiples (**didrachm, tridrachm, octadrachm, decadrachm, dodecadrachm**) and subdivision (**hemidrachm**) denoted coins of ½, 2, 3, 4, 8, 10 and 12 drachmae. These silver coins were minted all over the Greek world, the "owls" of Athens and the "foals" of Corinth being among the most popular trade coins of the Mediterranean in the pre-Christian era. Drachmae were also struck by the mints of the Alexandrine Empire and the Hellenistic kingdoms that followed, and imitated by the barbarian tribes of the Black Sea area and by the kingdoms of the Near and Middle East, whence they were adopted by the Arabs for the **dirhem** in the 13th century. Since 1831 the drachma has been the unit of currency in Greece (= 100 **lepta**), struck in silver till 1911 but subsequently in cupro-nickel (1926–73) and aluminium-bronze since 1973.

Dreibätzner   Coin worth 3 **batzen** or 12 **kreuzers**, struck in the 16th century by mints in southern Germany, Bohemia and Austria. In northern Germany similar coins were worth 4 **groschen**. Double pieces were also issued and were worth 6 batzen or 8 groschen respectively.

Dreier   From German for three, and signifying a coin worth 3 **pfennigs**, struck in northern Germany in the 16th–19th centuries in silver, but later in billon or copper.

Dreigröscher   Coin worth 3 **groschen**, first minted in 1528 under Sigismund I of Poland for circulation in Lithuania and subsequently in Prussia. Originally struck in silver, the precious metal was successively debased and by the late 16th century billon was used.

Dreiling   Name given to 3-**pfennig** coins struck by Hamburg, Lübeck and other north German cities in the 17th–19th centuries. At various times the dreiling was tariffed at 128 or 192 to the **taler**. The majority of dreilings were struck in billon but copper dreilings were struck at Altona (1787) and Kiel (1850) for use in Schleswig-Holstein.

Dreipetermännchen   Triple **petermännchen** worth 5 **kreuzers** and minted by the archbishopric of Trier in the 17th and 18th centuries.

Dreipölker   Small coin minted by Sigismund III of Poland for circulation in Silesia in the early 17th century, worth half a **dreigröscher**.

Dritteltaler   Silver coin worth a third of a **taler** or half a **silbergulden**.

Dub   Small coin of the Indian state of Hyderabad.

Dubbeltje   Dutch diminutive form of double, the popular name for the tiny 10-cent piece, originally worth two **stuivers**.

Ducat   Originally a silver coin struck in the Norman duchy (*ducatus*) of Apulia in the mid-12th century and modelled on contemporary Byzantine pieces, it was the inspiration of the silver **grosso** or ducato issued in Venice in 1202, the first important silver coin of multiple value to satisfy the growing needs of the European mercantile community. In 1284 Venice launched the *ducato d'oro* or gold ducat which derived its name from the reverse showing Christ and the legend *Sit t'xpe dat' q'tv regis iste dvcat* (May this duchy which Thou rulest be given to Thee, O Christ). So successful was this coin as a trade medium that ducat came to be synonymous with any small gold coin. From 1566 onwards it was the gold unit in the Holy Roman Empire and was produced under the authority of no fewer than 250 different principalities, duchies, cities and bishoprics, surviving in Austria as late as 1915. Ducats as trade coins were minted in Holland from 1586 till 1937.

Ducatone (ducatoon)   Name given to a silver coin worth three **guilders** or one gold **ducat**, minted in the Netherlands under Spanish or Austrian rule from 1618 to 1755, and to the Swedish 8-**mark** silver piece of 1644–1704.

Duetta   Copper coin of Tuscany, 16th–18th centuries, worth 2 **quattrini**, hence the name, a diminutive of *due* (two).

Duit   Tiny coin worth a quarter **groot** or an eighth of a **stuiver**. Struck in silver from the 14th century, it was reduced to copper in 1573. Latterly the duit was absorbed into the decimal system as the **cent**, and in this guise continues to this day. Duits and half-duits were struck by many of the Dutch provinces and also by the East India Company (with VOC monogram) at this rate of 100 or 120 to the **rupee**.

Dump   Popular name for any primitive coin struck on a very thick flan, but more specifically applied to the circular pieces cut from the centre of Spanish dollars, countermarked with the name of colony, a crown and the value, and circulated in New South Wales at 15 **pence** in 1813.
   See also **Holey Dollar**.

Dupondius   Roman bronze coin worth two **asses**, dating from the **Aes grave** period till the mid-3rd century A.D.

Dyak   Silver coin worth 2 **paisa**, issued in Nepal in the mid-18th century.

E

Eagle   United States 10-dollar gold piece, authorised in 1795 and minted till 1933, except for 1805–37. The name is derived from the American bald eagle depicted on the reverse. Half eagles were struck 1795–1929 and quarter eagles 1796–1929, while double eagles were issued from 1849 till 1933.

Ebenezer   Popular name given to the Danish **krone** of 1659, from the reverse motif showing the Ebenezer stone of health mentioned in the First Book of Samuel.

ECCA   Acronym signifying the Eastern Caribbean Currency Authority, responsible for the coins and paper notes issued in Antigua, Barbados, Dominica, Grenada, Montserrat, St. Christopher-Nevis-Anguilla, St. Lucia and St. Vincent.

Écu   French for escutcheon or heraldic shield and used to denote coins with this device. The first gold coin of this name appeared in 1266 and was known as the *écu d'or* or *denier à l'écu*. Later issues were known according to their principal motifs thus: *écu à la couronne* (crown), *à la croisette* (small cross), *au soleil* (sun), *au porc épic* (porcupine), *à la salamandre* (salamander), *à la perruque* (bewigged profile of Louis XIV), *aux lauriers* (laureated). The terms *écu blanc* or *écu d'argent* describe crown-sized silver coins of the 17th and 18th centuries. The *écu pistolet* was the first gold coin issued by the city of Geneva (1562–85).

ECU   European Currency Unit, a monetary unit proposed for use throughout the European Economic Community.

Edge inscription   Inscription on the edge of a coin or medal. An **incuse** inscription was applied to the edge of milled silver coins in the reign of Charles II, the Latin *Decus et Tutamen* (an ornament and a safeguard) alluding to the dual purpose – as a decoration and also to prevent clipping. Regnal dates appeared on the edge of some **crowns** of George III to Queen Victoria and a commemorative Latin inscription on the edge of the Festival of Britain crown (1951). Edge inscriptions, either raised or incuse, have appeared on many European coins, notably those of Germany and the Netherlands. Since 1979 the Isle of Man has issued heptagonal 50p coins with commemorative inscriptions on the edge – a very difficult feat to achieve technically. Incuse or raised inscriptions on the edges of military medals often give the number, rank, name and regiment or unit of the recipient – a practice which adds considerable personal interest to medal-collecting.

Edge ornament   Various devices applied to the edge of coins as a security device, to prevent clipping, date from the adoption of the milled pricess of production and are sometimes, though quite erroneously, referred to as **milling** but more properly as **reeding** or **graining**. This takes the form of a series of close vertical or diagonal serrations, but the more ornamental examples include tiny leaves, florets, interlocking rings, pellets and zigzag patterns.

Electrotype   Copy of a coin produced by electrolytically depositing a metallic shell against a mould taken from the original. This process is widely used in museums for security reasons.

Electrum   Alloy of gold and silver, sometimes called white gold, used for the minting of **staters** by the Asia Minor kingdom of Lydia in the 7th century B.C., the earliest example of coinage in the western world.

Elizabeth d'or   10-**rouble** gold coin of Tsarina Elizabeth II of Russia (1741–62).

Emergency money   Any form of money used in times of economic and political upheaval, when traditional kinds of currency are unavailable. Good examples are the comparatively crude silver coins issued by the Royalists at

Shrewsbury, Oxford and other cities during the Civil War (1642–9), **obsidional money**, issued in time of siege, from Leiden (1572) to Mafeking (1900), the **Notgeld** issued by many towns in Germany, 1916–23, **encased money, fractional currency, guerrilla notes, invasion, liberation** and **occupation money** from the two World Wars and minor campaigns. The most recent example of emergency money was the use of small **cheques** in Italy (1976–7) pending the introduction of new coins.

Enamelled coins   Coins decorated by enamelling the **obverse** and **reverse** motifs in contrasting colours, an art practised by jewellers in Birmingham and Paris in the 19th century, and recently revived in Europe and America. Favourite coins for this treatment included the Burmese peacock coins, British George and Dragon **crowns** and American **dollars**, but a host of smaller denominations, mainly those with armorial themes, were also treated in this way for incorporation in brooches, watch fobs, cuff-links and other jewellery.

Encased money   Postage stamps circulated as small change during a shortage of small coins in the American Civil War, and enclosed in small metal and mica-faced cases devised by John Gault of Boston. The face of the stamp was visible through the transparent window, while firms' advertisements could be embossed on the metal back. This practice was revived during and after the First World War when there was again a chronic shortage of small coins. Encased stamps have been recorded from France, Austria, Norway, Germany and Monaco.
See also **Postage Stamp Money**.

Engrailed   Term denoting a coin whose edge has some form of **reeding** or **graining** on it.

Engraving   The art of cutting lines or grooves in plates, blocks or dies. Numismatically this took the form of engraving images into the face of the **dies** used in striking coins, a process which has now been almost completely superseded by **hubbing** and the use of **reducing machinery**. In the production of paper money intaglio engraving is still commonly practised. In this process the engraver cuts the design into a steel die and the printing ink lies in the grooves. The paper is forced under great pressure into the grooves and picks up the ink, and this gives banknotes their characteristic ridged feeling to the touch. Nowadays many banknotes combine traditional intaglio engraving with multicolour lithography or photogravure to defeat the would-be forger.

Epigraphy   The study of inscriptions. When applied to **numismatics** this involves the classification and interpretation of coin **legends**, an invaluable adjunct to the study of a coin series, particularly the classical and medieval coins which, in the absence of dates and **mintmarks**, would otherwise be difficult to arrange in chronological sequence.

Erasion   The removal of the title or effigy of a ruler from the coinage issued after his or her death. This process was practised in Imperial Rome, and applied to coins of Caligula, Nero and Geta, as part of the more general practice of *damnatio memoriae* (damnation of the memory) ordered by the Senate.

Escudillo   Diminutive form of **escudo**, applied to the half-escudo, worth 10 **reales**, minted in Spain, 1746–1817.

Escudo   Spanish word for shield, from Latin *scutum*, applied to many gold or silver coins issued by Spain, Portugal and their respective overseas territories. The first coin of this name was a Spanish gold piece issued in 1537 as a successor to the **excelente**. The value fluctuated considerably and eventually the escudo had dwindled to a minor silver coin worth 2 **reales**. When the coinage was decimalised in 1866, the escudo was placed on par with the **real** and the **peseta** (= 100 **centimos**), but phased out by 1870. In Portugal the gold escudo was introduced in the 15th century but was generally inferior in precious metal content and value to its Spanish counterpart. Gold 2, 4 and 8 escudo coins were minted in the 18th century till 1828, but thereafter the escudo served as money of account until revived as the republican unit of currency in 1910 (= 100 **centavos**). Apart from the Portuguese overseas territories, the term escudo has also been applied to the gold pieces minted for use in Bolivia, Chile, Ecuador, Colombia, Peru and Uruguay in the 19th century, and was adopted by Chile as the unit of currency following the reform of 1960 (= 100 **centesimos**).

Espadin   **Billon** coin introduced by Alfonso V of Portugal in 1460. The name is derived from the word *espada* meaning a sword and alludes to the fact that the coin was originally intended to commemorate the foundation of the Military Order of the Tower and the Sword the previous year. The same type was retained under Joao III (1481–95) for the gold half **justo**.

Esphera   Gold half **cruzado** minted in Goa by authority of Alfonso de Albuquerque (1509–15), the first gold coin issued by a European colonial government. The coin takes its name from the sphere or globe of the world inscribed *mea* (half) – an allusion to the division of the New World between Spain and Portugal by the Treaty of Tordesillas, 1498.

Essay   From the French *essai*, a trial-piece. The term is applied to any piece struck for the purposes of examination by parliamentary or financial bodies, prior to the authorisation of an issue of coins or paper money. The official nature of these items distinguishes them from **patterns**, which denote trial pieces often produced by mints or even private individuals bidding for coinage contracts.

Esterling   Archaic form of sterling, used for medieval silver pennies of guaranteed excellence. The name is popularly derived from the north German merchants, or 'Easterlings', who came to England in the reign of Edward I (1272–1307) and formed a guild in London. Their coins were of uniform weight and fineness, according to a statement by Walter de Pinchbeck, although the word occurs in its French form (*esterlin*) in the late 11th century. Other theories of the etymology of the world will be found under **sterling.**

Excelente   Gold coin, first minted under Ferdinand and Isabella in 1497 as the Spanish counterpart of the **ducat**, and a prototype for the *doubloons* which were so popular as international trade coins in the early modern period.

Exergue   Lower segment of a coin or medal, usually divided from the rest of the field by a horizontal line, and often containing the date, value, ornament or identification symbols.

Eyrir (plural **aurar**)   The Icelandic unit of currency equivalent of öre. 100 **aurar** = 1 **krona**.

F

Faluce   Small copper coin issued in Ceylon during the Dutch administration. 4 faluce = 1 **fanam**.

Falus (fals, fels, fols)   Arabic name for a copper coin, derived from the Roman and Byzantine **follis** and in turn leading to the **fils** which serves as a unit of currency in many Arab countries to this day. Cast brass falus were issued by the Sherifian government of Morocco in the 19th century.

Fanam   Unit of currency in southern India, derived from the Hindi *panam*, meaning a handful, and originally alluding to a handful of seed corn. In coinage the fanam was the largest silver piece, and also the smallest gold coin. Gold fanams date from the Tamil kingdoms of the 10th century, spreading thence to Travancore and Ceylon in the 14th century. Silver fanams date from the 16th and 17th centuries and were struck by the European powers for circulation in their respective territories. The British tariffed the fanam at eight to the **rupee**, whereas the French had five to the rupee.

Fano   Small silver coin issued at Tranquebar (Danish settlements in India), 1730–1818.

Fantasy coins   Pieces of metal, often in gold or silver, purporting to be the coinage of countries which do not exist. Recent examples include the money inscribed for use in Atlantis and the coins struck on behalf of the principality of the Hutt Valley whose ruler, Prince Leonard, has declared his independence from Western Australia.

FAO coins   Coins issued by many countries to publicise, and raise funds for, the Food and Agricultural Organisation of the United Nations. The programme began in 1968 and to date coins have been issued by countries in every part of the world, mainly in the developing nations of the Third World. The coins depict aspects of agriculture, fisheries and food production and often bear the FAO slogan "Food for All", or its equivalent in other languages. The FAO programme was the first attempt at international cooperation in issuing coins with a common theme and, while aimed at collectors, the coins are predominantly low-denomination circulating issues designed to educate the public in the countries themselves. More recent coins in the FAO programme have widened their message to include family planning. So far Jamaica is the only country to issue a banknote for the FAO programme. The FAO itself also sponsors a series of medals honouring famous women, past and present, the Ceres programme taking its name from the Roman corn goddess.

Farthing   In English money the quarter of a penny, deriving its name from "fourthling". The earliest farthings were, in fact, silver **pennies** cut into four parts, but small coins of this value were struck in silver in the reign of Edward I (1272–1307) and silver **threefarthing** coins were minted in the reign of Elizabeth I from 1561 to 1582. The last silver farthing was minted about 1550, but copper farthings were produced under royal licence by Lord **Harington** in the reign of James I (1603–25). The first regal base-metal farthings appeared in 1672. Copper or tin was used at first, then copper from 1695 till 1859 and bronze from 1860 till 1956 when this virtually worthless denomination was discontinued.

Fei-chen   Chinese for "flying-money", an apt term for the world's first paper money produced during the T'ang Dynasty (A.D. 650–800). Chinese merchants devised these paper drafts, negotiable in bronze **cash**, as a means of overcoming the transportation of the cumbersome coins. Though not authorised by the state they paved the way for the paper money introduced by the Sung Dynasty about A.D. 1000 which were redeemable in coin.

Fen   Originally a bronze coin issued by the Communists in Manchuria, 1933–4, it was adopted as the unit of currency by the People's Republic of China. Aluminium coins of 1, 2 and 5 fen have been minted since 1955 (100 = 1 **yüan**).

Fenig (plural **fenigow**)   Polish version of the German **pfennig**, inscribed on subsidiary coins issued by the German occupation administration of Poland during the First World War. After the German withdrawal in 1917, iron or zinc coins of 1 to 20 fenigow were issued by the provisional government of the Polish republic.

Feorling   Gaelic for **farthing**, inscribed on Irish farthings, 1928–66.

Ferding   Swedish word for **farthing**. Silver quarter-mark coin first issued in Livonia in 1516 and struck at Reval during the Swedish occupation (1561–70). Similar coins were minted in Dorpat and Ösel in the mid-16th century. Ferdings of Riga in the 17th century were tariffed at 24 to the reichstaler.

Field   Flat part of the surface of a coin or medal, between the **legend**, the effigy and other raised parts of the design.

Filiberto   Gold and silver coins of Savoy, issued under Philibert I (1553–80).

Filippo (Felippo)   Spanish silver coin issued in the reign of Philip II (1556–98) for use in northern Italy and tariffed at 100 **soldi**.

Filler   Magyar equivalent of the Austrian **heller**, forming the Hungarian unit of currency since 1892. Originally 100 to the **korona**, then 100 to the **pengö** (1926) and 100 to the **forint** since 1946.

Fils   Unit of currency in Bahrain (1,000 = 1 **dinar**), Iraq (1,000 = 1 dinar), Jordan (100 = 1 dinar), Kuwait (1,000 = 1 dinar) and South Arabia (1,000 = 1 dinar), derived from the Byzantine and Roman **follis** and the medieval Arab **fels**.

Fiorino   Originally a silver coin, but later struck in gold, by the city of Florence from about 1220. The name was a pun on the principal device, a little flower (*fiore*) from which the city derived its own name. The silver coin was worth a **soldo**, while the gold coin was worth a **lira**. The gold fiorino soon became one of the leading trade coins of the late Middle Ages and the model for the gold coins of other states. Double fiorini were minted between 1504 and 1531.

Flan   Alternative name for **blank** or **planchet**, the piece of metal struck between **dies** to produce a coin or medal.

Fleur de Coin   French term, often abbreviated as FDC, signifying a coin in the very finest condition and specifically reserved in France to denote a proof piece.

Flitter   Smaller copper coin circulating in southern Germany in the 17th century and worth half a **pfennig**. Coins worth 2, 3 and 4 flitter were also struck during the Thirty Years War (1618–48). The term is also used loosely in modern German parlance to denote tinsel or spangles on circus costume.

Florin   Name given to coins issued in several European countries, modelled on the **fiorino** of Florence. The first of these imitations was the florin struck by Philippe IV of France in 1290, rapidly emulated by the semi-independent mints in various parts of France and it was from Aquitaine that the gold florin spread to England in 1344, otherwise known as the double **leopard** of 6 **shillings**. The earliest German florins were struck by the Hanseatic League in 1340 but soon spread to the Rhineland and the archbishoprics of Mainz, Trier and Cologne, the duchies of Jülich and Guelders and the county of Cleves. Florins spread to southern Germany by the late 14th century. The first gold coins of Central Europe were florins struck at Kremnitz in 1324 and by 1340 they were being minted in Hungary, Bohemia, Austria and Silesia. The florin suffered from over-imitation, and the debasement of Aragonese florins gave this coin a bad image. By the end of the 15th century it had been largely superseded by the **ducat** and the doubloon as a trade coin. The name, however, survived in the Netherlands as a synonym for the silver **gulden** or **guilder**, and to this day the notation for Dutch guilders is *Fl*. The name was revived in Britain in 1849 to signify a silver coin worth two shillings, introduced as the first stage in **decimalisation** and inscribed ONE FLORIN/ONE TENTH OF A POUND. Later issues were inscribed ONE FLORIN/TWO SHILLINGS. The term florin was used on its own on the coins of George V (1911–36) but the inscription TWO SHILLINGS was substituted on the coins of George VI and Queen

Elizabeth (1937–67) and the term "florin" gradually died out. Its present equivalent is the decimal 10 penny piece, Silver florins were also issued in Australia, British East Africa, Ireland (spelled floirin), Malawi, New Zealand, Rhodesia and Nyasaland and South Africa.

Follis (Plural **folles**)   Roman bronze coin with a silver wash, adopted as part of the monetary reforms of Diocletian (A.D. 295). Due to inflation the follis quickly superseded the silver **denarius** in general circulation and was minted in vast quantities. Thereafter the follis was successively devalued and reduced in size. The name was also used for a copper coin issued in the Byzantine Empire, from the reign of Anastasius onwards, and was worth 40 **nummi**.

Forint   Magyar word for **florin**, and originally the gold coin of that denomination minted in Hungary in the 14th century. It was revived as a silver coin worth 100 **krajczar** (1857–92) and has been the principal unit of currency since 1946, worth 100 **filler**.

Fractional currency   Emergency issue of small-denomination notes by the United States in 1863–5, following a shortage of coins caused by the Civil War. They superseded the **Postage Currency** notes but bore the inscription 'Receivable for all U.S. stamps', alluding to the most popular medium of small change at that time. Denominations ranged from 3 to 50¢.

Franc   French coin, originally struck in gold as the *franc à cheval* (1360) on account of the equestrian figure depicted on it. It was followed by the *franc à pied*, portraying Charles V on foot, and subsequent gold francs were minted in the 15th century. The first silver franc appeared in 1577 under Henri III. Thereafter the word franc was used as money of account, on par with the **livre**, but was revived as an actual coin in 1793, worth 100 **centimes**. This system has continued to the present day. For much of the intervening period the franc was a silver coin, about the size of an English **shilling**, but at various times it has been struck in aluminium-bronze (1931–41), aluminium (1941–59) or pure nickel (since 1960), reflecting the vagaries of the French currency in recent times. By contrast, 5- and 10-franc coins were struck in silver for general circulation as recently as 1969 and 1973 respectively. Gold 10- and 20-franc coins were struck till 1914 and gold 100-franc coins in 1935–6. The franc is also the unit of currency in many former French colonies, and has been used by Belgium (since 1831), Luxembourg (since 1854) and Switzerland since the early 19th century, some cantonal issues being inscribed with the German or Italian equivalents – *franken* or *franchi*.

Francescone   Silver **scudo** of Tuscany, minted under Francesco I (1574–87), and later used for the scudo of 10 **paoli** struck by authority of Francis III of Lorraine for use in Etruria (1737).

Franco (plural **franchi**)   Silver coin issued in the Italian duchy of Lucca under French occupation (1805–8) and portraying Elisa Bonaparte (Napoleon's sister) and her consort, Felix Bacciochi.

Frang   Letzeburgish word for **franc**, inscribed on the 5-franc coin of Luxembourg (1949) and various denominations of paper money.

Franka Ari   Albanian for gold **frank**, the principal unit of currency adopted in Albania in 1925 on joining the **Latin Monetary Union**. It was worth 5 **lek** or 500 **qindarka**. Coins of 1, 2 and 5 franka ari were struck in silver and 10 and 20 franka ari in gold.

Franklinium   Cupro-nickel alloy developed by the Franklin Mint of Philadelphia and used for coins, medals and gaming tokens since 1967.

Frederik d'or   Danish gold coin struck in the reigns of Frederik VI and Frederik VII, between 1827 and 1863 at the Altona and Copenhagen mints.

Frosting   Matt surface used for the high relief area of many proof coins and medals, to give greater contrast with the mirrored surface of the field.

Fuang   Thai word, from Malay *wang* meaning "coin", used to denote a small silver coin worth an eighth of a **tical** or

baht, struck by Taylor & Challen of Birmingham for King Mongkut (1851–68). Even smaller denominations, down to a sixteenth of a fuang, were struck in copper or a tin alloy until 1908.

Fugio cent   First officially authorised coin of the United States, struck in 1787. The word "**cent**" did not appear on the pieces, which were undenominated, but some 300 tons of copper were coined to provide small change. They were struck at New Haven, Connecticut, and may also have been minted in New York and Rupert, Vermont. The name comes from the motto *Fugio* on the obverse, signifying that time flies. The mottoes "Mind your business" and "we are one" appear in the obverse **exergue** and the centre of the reverse respectively, and are said to have been put forward by Benjamin Franklin. The copper is believed to have come from the bands of powder kegs supplied by the French to the American rebels during the War of Independence.

Fun   Unit of currency in the Korean Empire. Copper 5-fun coins were issued in 1894.

Funeral Money   Imitations of banknotes and other paper money, used in China and Latin America in funeral ceremonies. Chinese **hell notes** are buried with the dead so that they may pay for food and services when they pass over to the next world. In many parts of Europe from classical times actual coins are placed on the eyes of the corpse and buried for the same purpose.

Fyrk (plural **fyrkar**)   From Swedish *fyrken*, diminutive of *fyr* (four). Name given to a small silver coin worth 4 **pfennig** minted from 1478. Copper fyrkar were struck in 1624–5 and in **klippe** form in 1627–9. Quarter-**öre** coins with this name were also minted in 1633–60.

G

Gabellone Large silver coin of the 16th and 17th centuries, minted in Bologna with a value of 26 **bolognini**. A similar coin of the Papal States (*c*. 1634–43) was tariffed at 30 bolognini, 3 **bianchi** or 1.5 **lire**.

Galvanoplasty Alternative term for the process of making **electrotype** copies of coins.

Gayah Malay word for elephant, denoting a cast tin coin of Sumatra in the 18th and 19th centuries which depicted that animal.

Gazetta Copper coin issued by the Venetian Republic in the 17th and 18th centuries for circulation in the Ionian Islands and Crete.

Geat (git) Channel through which molten metal is ducted to the mould. Cast coins and medals often show tiny protrusions known as geat marks.

Genovino Gold coins of Genoa, first minted in 1150 but later copied by Florence and Venice. From the late 16th century it was also struck in silver on par with the **scudo**.

George Noble Rare English gold coin struck under Henry VIII in 1526–33 and tariffed at a third of a pound or 6s. 8d. It took its name from the reverse motif of St. George and the Dragon. A half george noble was also struck, but only one example is known to have survived.

Georgstaler Large silver coin depicting St. George and the Dragon, struck by several German principalities in the 16th and 17th centuries, and popular with soldiers as a lucky piece, especially during the Thirty Years War (1618–48).

German Silver (also known in German as *Neusilber*, 'new silver')   Alloy of copper, zinc and nickel providing a base-metal substitute for silver and used for the 10 and 20 **rappen** of Switzerland (1850–77), the Austrian 10 **heller** and Hungarian 10 **filler** (1915–16).

Gigliato   Silver coin deriving its name from the profusion of fleur de lys (*gigli*) on the reverse. First issued at Naples in 1303 by Charles II of Anjou, it was struck in vast quantities to finance Angevin adventures in Italy and was soon copied by the Pope at Avignon and by the princes of the Rhone valley. It served as the model for the papal **carlino** and was also struck at Kremnitz in Hungary. The gigliato was copied by the Crusaders in Rhodes and Cyprus and by the Turcoman emirs of Ionia.

Gigot   Copper coin of Brabant worth half a **liard**, minted in Antwerp and Bruges under Francis of Anjou during the campaign for the liberation of the Spanish Netherlands, 1581. Gigots were also struck in the 17th century at Bois-le-Duc ('s-Hertogenbosch), Mons and Reckheim for local circulation.

Giorgino   Billon coin worth a **grosso**, struck in Ferrara during the reign of Alfonso d'Este (1559–97), and subsequently in Modena under Cesare d'Este (1598–1628). It derived its name from the reverse motif of St. George and the Dragon.

Giovannino   Italian for "little John", the name given to the small coin worth 5 **soldi** issued in late 17th century Genoa, with the effigy of St. John.

Glass money   Glass beads are known to have been used as a form of currency in Egypt and Phoenicia in pre-Christian times, and in many parts of Africa, Asia, the Pacific islands and America from the earliest days of European colonisation. These beads were strung together, often in intricate patterns and fine examples are highly regarded as currency curiosa.

Godless Florin   Nickname of the first British silver florin (1849) because the abbreviation D.G. (*Dei Gratia* – by the grace of God) was omitted.

Gold Precious metal, atomic symbol and numismatic abbreviation *Au*, from the Latin *Aurum*. Gold has been used as a coinage metal since the 7th century B.C., both as an alloy with silver (*electrum*) or in its more or less pure form. Although 24 carat or 1.000 fine gold has been used for medals and a few proof coins, this is too soft to be practical for circulating gold, and a small admixture of silver or copper is usual. In England fine gold was deemed as 23¾ carat, reduced in the reign of Henry VIII (1509–47) to 22 carat (1526) but thereafter fluctuated between 23 carat and 20 carat (1544), raised again to 22 carat (1549) and 23 carat (1553) before settling at "crown gold" standard of 22 carat or .916 fineness in the reign of Elizabeth I. European gold coins have fluctuated between .986 and .900 fine, but in recent years some gold coins have been struck at .500, .400 or even .375 (9 carat) fineness. Medals have been minted in pure gold, but 18, 12 or 9 carat gold is more common. Many of the great coins of history were produced as a convenient method of handling gold: the **ducat**, **florin**, **aureus**, **tremissis**, doubloon, **joe**, **napoleon**, **eagle** and **sovereign**, down to the **krugerrand** of the present day.

Golde Nominal unit of currency in Sierra Leone, worth 50 **leones**. Gold quarter, half and 1 golde coins were issued in 1966.

Goldgulden German name for gold coins modelled on the **fiorino**, minted in the 14th century and paving the way for the **gulden**.

Goldpfennig Gold penny minted sporadically in medieval Germany from the reign of Charlemagne to the time of Frederick II, on a ratio of one to 20 silver pennies. Similar attempts to produce gold pence in England resulted in Mercian copies of Arab **dinars** and the unique gold penny of Offa (*c.* 780), but these experiments were obviously abortive, as were the experiments of Henry III (1257) with a gold penny, twice the weight of silver and worth 20 times as much.

Gong money Cast bronze bells and gongs used as currency in many parts of Asia, notably Burma where such pieces were known as **Kyee-zee** and were worth from 100 to 1,000

rupees. Gong money has been recorded as far afield as West Africa and the Sunda Islands.

Goodfor   Popular name for **token** coins and **emergency money** made of paper or card, from the inscription "Good for . . ." followed by a monetary value. They have been recorded from Europe, America and Africa in times of economic crises or shortage of more traditional coinage.

Gothic Crown   Popular name for the silver **crown** of the United Kingdom, 1847–53, so-called because of the legend in Gothic script.

Gourde   French for gourd, the large succulent fruit of the genus *Cucurbita*. In the French West Indies in the 18th century gourds were a popular form of barter currency worth a **piastre**, and this was adapted by Henri Christophe, ruler of Haiti (1806–11) as the unit of currency, striking silver gourdes worth 5 **francs**. Silver gourdes were minted by his successors and the gourde is the Haitian unit of currency to this day (= 100 **centimes**).

Grain   The weight of a single grain of wheat was taken as the smallest unit of weight in England. The **troy grain** was 1/5,760 of a pound, while the avoirdupois grain was 1/7,000 of a pound, the former being used in the weighing of precious metal and thus employed by numismatists in weighing coins. A grain is 1/480 troy ounce or 1/15 gram in the metric system.

Graining   Term sometimes used as a synonym for the **reeding** on the edge of milled coins.

Gramo   Spanish word for gramme, used by Julius Popper for 1- and 5-gramo gold coins, minted in 1889 for nominal circulation in Tierra del Fuego, following the discovery of vast deposits of alluvial gold there. The expression also appeared on the reverse of the copper coins issued by the Spanish provisional government (1870).

Grano   Small copper coin struck in southern Italy and tariffed at 100 to the gold **ducat**. The first appeared in Naples and Sicily in 1460 and spread to Malta where it survived till the mid-19th century, being superseded by the diminutive third-farthing of Queen Victoria minted between 1844 and 1885.

Grenadino   8-real silver piece struck for use in the republic of New Granada (1837–47), later renamed Colombia.

Griffon (gryphon)   Base-silver coin of Brabant, issued in the 15th century and worth a **stuiver**.

Gripped edge   Term denoting the pattern of indentations found on the majority of American cents of 1797, caused by the **milling** process. Coins of the same date with a plain edge are rather scarcer.

Grivenka   Russian unit of weight used for precious metals, equivalent to the **mark** in western Europe. The term was a diminutive form of **grivna** and signified half its weight.

Grivennik   Russian 10-**kopek** coin, struck in silver from the reign of Peter the Great till 1936 but in cupro-nickel since then.

Grivna (plural grivny)   Russian unit of weight adopted in the 13th century, derived from the gold necklaces which were a form of primitive currency from the 10th century onwards. In the 13th and 14th centuries the grivna was a silver ingot which circulated as money. It was also the unit of currency in the short-lived Ukrainian Republic (1918–23).

Groat   English silver coin worth 4 **pence**, based on the French **gros**, introduced by Edward I in 1279 and struck for general circulation intermittently until 1855. Groats dated 1888 were also minted for use in British Guiana (Guyana). The groat survives to this day, however, as the silver four-penny coin in the **Maundy** series. In the period up to 1836 the groat and Maundy fourpence were virtually synonymous but from that date groats for general circulation had a Britannia reverse, whereas the Maundy coin had a numeral design. Groats were also struck in Scotland from 1357 onwards but varied in value, from 4 pence to 8 pence (1526) and latterly to 12 pence (1558), originally in silver but latterly in billon.

Groot   Silver coin of the Netherlands, based on the French **gros**, issued first in the reign of John II of Brabant

(1294–1312) but later circulating in other provinces. Its debasement led to the double **groot**, also known as the **botdrager**.

Gros   French word for fat, from Latin *grossus* or *crassus*. Silver coin introduced by Louis IX of France in 1262 as part of the monetary reforms aimed at reducing the power of the feudal coinage and strengthening the central coinage. Louis took as his standard the coins minted by the abbey of St. Martin at Tours, 12 **deniers tournois** being worth one gros tournois. This was the first large silver coin in Europe since classical times and paved the way for the **groat**, **grosso** and other multiples of the **penny** adopted in other countries, from the British Isles to the Crusader kingdoms. Though later replaced by the **sol** or **sou** in France, its influence is reflected in the wide range of coins whose names are derived from it.

Grosch (**Grush, gersh, girsh, guerche, grosch**)   Small coins of eastern Europe, the Near and Middle East derived from the **gros**. Originally a copper coin worth 2 **kopeks** (1724–7) it spread to the Ottoman Empire and its variants emerged in different areas as grosh or grush (Balkans and Turkey), girsh (Hejaz-Nejd, Saudi Arabia), guerche (Egypt) and thence to Ethiopia as girsh. The modern Turkish **kurus** is derived from this term.

Groschen   German word, originally signifying "little **grosso**", borrowed by the mints of southern Germany from the grosso circulating in northern Italy from the late 12th century. To exploit the silver deposits of Kuttenberg (Kutna Hora) east of Prague, Wenceslas II of Bohemia established a mint there in 1298 and began striking silver coins inscribed "Grossi Pragensis" on the reverse, hence their name of Prager groschen. It circulated widely in Europe and was much imitated, particularly in Saxony, Hesse and Poland. By the 16th century the groschen, in various guises, was the most popular unit of currency all over the Germanic area. The reichsgroschen, **gutegroschen** or **mariengroschen** was tariffed at 24 to the **taler**. In the 19th century the **silbergroschen** was worth 12 **pfennigs**, while the neugroschen of Saxony was worth 10 pfennigs. To this day the 10 pfennig coin in Germany is popularly known as a groschen. Since 1925 the groschen has been the unit of currency in Austria, at the rate of 100 to the **schilling**.

Grossetto   Diminutive form of the Italian word **grosso**, first used for the half value coin issued at Venice in the 15th century. Subsequently it was used to denote the greatly debased grossi produced in Venice for use in the Adriatic and Levantine area.

Grosso (plural **grossi**)   Italian word for big and first used to denote the double **soldo** issued by Venice in 1202. Thereafter its value fluctuated between 14 and 24 **denari**. The grosso was soon imitated in other parts of Italy and was the inspiration for the French **gros** and the German **groschen**.

Grossone   Silver coin struck in many parts of Italy till the late 18th century, derived from the earlier **grosso**.

Grosspfennig   Silver coin minted in many parts of Germany from the early 14th century onwards. Its value varied considerably. In the Rhineland it was worth 2½ **pfennigs**, in Pomerania 6 Lübeck pfennigs, and marked the transition from the medieval penny system to the groschen standard of the early modern period.

Grosz (plural **groszy**)   Polish unit of currency, formerly 24 to the **taler** but since 1923 100 groszy = 1 **zloty**.

Grote   Unit of currency in the Hanseatic city of Bremen, prior to its absorption into the North German Confederation in 1867. It was first minted in the late 15th century, being worth two-thirds of a **schilling**, 72 to the **taler**, 32 to the **mark** or 36 to the **gulden**.

Guarani   Unit of current in Paraguay since 1944 (= 100 **centimos**). Steel coins in denominations from 1 to 50 guaranis have been struck since 1974.

Guerrilla notes   Paper money issued in areas under the control of guerrillas and partisans during wartime range from the **veld ponds** of the Boers (1900–2) to the notes issued by the Garibaldi Brigade in Italy and the anti-fascist notes of Yugoslavia. The most prolific issues were those produced in Luzon, Mindanao and Negros Occidental by the Filipino resistance during the Japanese occupation (1942–5).

Guilder see **Gulden**

Guilloche   French term signifying the intricate pattern of curved lines produced by the rose engine and used as a security feature in banknote printing.

Guinea   British gold coin, first minted in 1663 in the reign of Charles II with a value of 20 **shillings**, rising to 30 shillings in 1695, dropping to 21.5 shillings in 1696 and finally settling at 21 shillings in 1717. The name was derived from the African coast of Guinea whence came the gold imported by the African Company whose emblem, the elephant and castle, appeared below the king's profile on the **obverse**. Half- and third-guineas were produced in 1669–1813 and 1797–1813 respectively, while quarter-guineas were minted in 1718 and 1762 during shortages of silver. Multiples of 2 and 5 guineas dated from 1664 and 1668 respectively and continued intermittently till 1753 but the very rare coins portraying George III and dated between 1768 and 1777 were only patterns. The guinea as an actual coin was superseded by the **sovereign** in 1816 but survived as money of account till the advent of decimalisation in 1971.

Gulden   Corruption of the word "golden", applied in the German-speaking areas of Europe to the gold trade coins based on the **fiorino** and the **ducat**, but from the mid-14th century used to denote gold coins struck at numerous German mints. Later on, as silver supplanted gold as the principal medium for coinage, the term was retained as money of account and lent itself to several large silver coins, such as the **guldiner**, the **guldengroschen** and the **silbergulden**. From the 18th to the late 19th century the gulden was the principal unit of currency in Austria and the south German states, and survives to this day as the unit of currency in the Netherlands and associated overseas territories, worth 100 **cents**. From 1923 till 1939 the gulden of 100 **pfennigs** was the unit of currency in the Free city of Danzig.

Guldengroschen   Synonym for the imperial **taler** in the northern and northwestern German states in the late 15th and early 16th centuries, based on the Rhenish **gulden**. Large silver coins of this name were first minted by Sigismund of the

Tirol in 1486 and spread as far as Hungary, but were superseded by the **taler** after 1519.

Guldiner   South German counterpart of the **gulden-groschen**, used also in Austria and Switzerland, before the advent of the **taler** in the 1520s.

Gunmetal   Bronze alloy obtained by melting down **cannon**. It was used in Ireland during the Williamite War (1689–91) for the **emergency coinage** produced by supporters of James II in denominations from the **sixpence** to the **crown**. It is also used to this day in the manufacture of the Victoria Cross, Britain's highest award for bravery, from Russian cannon captured during the Crimean War (1853–6).

Gun money   Name given to the Irish **emergency coinage** of 1689–91 minted from **gunmetal**.

Gutegroschen   Small coin circulating in north and central districts of Germany and tariffed at 24 to the **taler**. It was superseded by the **mariengrosschen** tariffed at 36 to the taler.

Gutschein   German word for voucher or coupon, denoting the paper money used aboard ships of the Imperial Germany Navy during the First World War, from the inscription *Gutschein* followed by the name of the ship. The last issue was made at Scapa Flow, 1918–19 during the internment of the navy.

H

Halala Small bronze or aluminium coin of the Yemen, worth half a **bogash**.

Haler (plural forms **haleru, halerzy** or **halierov**) Unit of currency in Czechoslovakia, cf. Austrian **heller**, used since 1921. 100 haleru = 1 **koruna**.

Halfpenny As half of the medieval silver **penny**, a silver coin minted first by the Vikings of East Anglia in the late 9th century, and by Alfred the Great at London. Silver halfpence continued intermittently until the outbreak of the Civil War (1642) and the Commonwealth (*c*. 1650) but tin, copper or bronze were used for later issues down to the present day. The majority of the **tokens** of the 17th–19th centuries consisted of copper halfpence.

Haller Original name for the **heller**, derived from Hall in Swabia where this small coin was first minted. This spelling survived in Switzerland till the late 18th century.

Hammered coins Term denoting coins produced by the traditional method of striking a **flan** laid on an anvil with a hammer. Originally the device was engraved directly on to the striking face of the hammer but later, to save wear and tear, the device was engraved on a separate **die** which was then hit by a hammer on to the blank. A characteristic of hammered coins was their uneven shape, which tended to encourage **clipping**. The advent of the screw press in the 15th century, and the mechanisation of coining processes due to **milling** in the 16th and 17th centuries, led to the demise of hammering, but it survived at the Royal Mint, London as late as 1662, largely due to the intransigence of mint officials and their workforce.

Hao   Alternative name for the **dong** or **piastre** of Annam and Vietnam.

Hard head   Billon Scottish coin worth 1½ pence, introduced by Mary Queen of Scots in 1555 and based on the French **hardi**. It was raised to 2 **pence** under James VI and contined till 1660.

Hardi   Coins struck in gold (*d'or*) or silver (*d'argent*) by Edward the Black Prince during the Hundred Years War in imitation of the *masse d'or* of Philippe le Hardi, King of France, hence the name. Gold hardis were also minted under Richard II and Henry V in the 15th century. Silver hardis were struck in France under Louis XI, Charles VII and Louis XII in the 16th century. The name was also given to the coins minted at Turin early in the 16th century during the French occupation.

Hard Times Token   Copper piece the size of the large **cent**, issued in the United States between 1834 and 1844. A vendetta waged by President Andrew Jackson against the Bank of the United States led to its collapse. This in turn precipitated the panic of 1837 and the economic crisis of 1839, the landmarks in a period known as the Hard Times. Banks suspended **specie** payments and the shortage of coin was filled by **tokens** issued by tradesmen. Many of these tokens were more in the nature of satirical **medalets** than circulating pieces.

Harington Token   Base-metal **farthing** produced by Lord Harington in 1613, under licence from James I, to meet demands from the public for subsidiary coinage. The franchise later passed to the Duke of Lennox.

Hat Piece   Alternative name for the **bonnet piece** of James VI of Scotland, 1591.

Hau   Tongan unit of currency worth 100 **pa'anga**. Quarter, half and 1 hau coins were minted in palladium in 1967.

Hekte   Greek for sixth, an **electrum** coin of Lesbos and Mytilene worth a sixth of a **stater**.

Heller   Originally a lightweight version of the **pfennig**, minted under Frederick I of Hohenstaufen at Hall in Swabia, it gradually spread to other parts of Austria and southern Germany by the late 13th century, but thereafter it became debased and was eventually worth only half a pfennig. Multiple hellers were also struck in the Rhineland. The heller was revived in southern Germany in the 19th century as an eighth **kreuzer** and was adopted by Austria in 1892 for the decimal system of 100 heller to the **krone** which continued till 1916.

Hell notes   Imitation paper money used in Chinese funeral ceremonies and buried with the dead to pay for services in the next world.

Hemi   Greek prefix meaning half, found in coins such as the *hemiassarion* (half **as**) minted by some Greek cities under Roman imperial rule, the *hemidrachm* (half **drachma**) of the Greek and Hellenistic period, the *hemihekton* (half **hekte**), *hemilitron* (half **litra**) of Sicily, the *hemiobol* (half **obol**), and the *hemitetartemorion* (literally half a quarter part) the smallest coin of the Greek states, worth an eighth of an obol.

Henri d'or (**Henri à la Gallia**)   The first gold coin in the world to be produced by the screw press. The 23 carat henri, slightly heavier than the **écu**, portrayed Henri II, hence its name. The alternative name comes from the allegorical female figure of Gallia (France) depicted on the reverse. Experiments with milled coinage began in 1552 and led to the henri three years later.

Hoard   Accumulation of coins concealed in times of economic or political upheaval and discovered, often centuries later. Under English common law such hoards are subject to the law of **treasure trove** if they contain precious metal. The advent of metal detectors has in recent years brought numerous hoards of classical and medieval coins to light in every part of Europe from Scandinavia to the Mediterranean.

Hog Money (**Hogge Money, Hoggies**)   Popular name for the earliest coinage of Bermuda (Sommer Islands). This coinage, the first struck for the British colonies in America, was issued about 1616. The coins were minted in brass with a silver wash and comprised twopence, three-pence, sixpence and shilling. The name is derived from the hog depicted on each obverse, with the value expressed in Roman numerals. Pigs are thought to have been put on Bermuda in 1515 by Juan Bermudez and when Sir George Somers was shipwrecked there in 1609 his crew found them a welcome source of food. This incident served as the basis for Shakespeare's play *The Tempest*, which refers to "the still vex'd Bermoothes".

Holed coins   Term used to denote two quite different categories: (a) coins which have been pierced for suspension as a form of jewellery or talisman, and (b) coins which have a hole as part of their design. In the first category a notable example is the English medieval gold **angel** which was regarded as an amulet against scrofula or king's evil. Many eastern gold or silver coins were pierced for wear by the owner. Coins with a hole in their design include the Chinese **cash**, with its distinctive square hole, many of the colonial coins of the Congo, Dutch East Indies, and British West and East Africa, and numerous minor coins from Europe (Belgium, Denmark, Finland, France, Hungary, Norway and Spain). Among the Asiatic countries India, Japan, Nepal and Syria have issued holed coins. In the case of India the 1 **pice** bronze coin of 1943–7 has such a large hole that the surrounding metal is barely large enough to bear the inscription.

Holey dollar   Spanish silver piece of 8 **reales** with the centre removed. The resultant "ring" was countermarked "New South Wales" and dated 1813, with "Five Shillings" on the reverse and placed into circulation during a shortage of British coin. The centre piece, known as a **dump**, was circulated at 15 pence.

Hub   Heavy circular piece of steel on which the **die** for a coin or medal is engraved. The process of cutting the die and transferring the master die, by means of intermediary punches, to the die from which coins will be struck is known as hubbing. Soft steel is used in the preliminary process, and after the design has been transferred, the hub is hardened by chemical means.

Hvid (Danish for white)   A small coin, originally in silver but later in billon, worth 4 pfennig or a third of a skilling, minted between 1370 and 1686.

Hwan   Originally a silver coin of the Korean Empire, but also used in 1959–66 as the unit of currency with South Korea.

Hybrid   see Mule

Hyperpyron   Byzantine gold coin introduced by Alexius I in 1092.

I

Ichibu-gin   Rectangular silver piece worth 1 **bu**, circulating as currency in Japan, 1837–69.

Imadi   Unit of currency of the Yemen from 1923 till 1962, but since superseded by the **ryal** (= 40 **bogash**). Circular half and quarter imadis and five-sided one-eighth and one-sixteenth imadis were minted in the same period.

Imitation money   Also known as play money or toy money, it consists of coins and notes produced for games of chance, children's toy shops and post offices, as tourist souvenirs or political satire (e.g. the shrinking pound or dollar). See also **funeral money**, **hell notes**, **model coins** and **skit notes**.

Imperial   Russian 10-**rouble** gold coin, introduced by the Tsarina Elizabeth in 1755.

Incuse   Impression which cuts into the surface of a coin or medal, as opposed to the more usual raised relief. Many of the earliest coins, especially those with a device on one side only, bear an incuse impression, often in a geometric pattern. An incuse impression appears on one side of **bracteate** coins, reflecting the relief image of the other side. Few coins of modern times have an incuse design, but notable examples were the American half **eagle** and quarter eagle gold coins of 1908–29 designed by Bela Pratt.

Inflation money   Coins produced as a result of inflation date back to Roman times when bronze **minimi** little bigger than a pinhead circulated as **denarii**. Nearer the present day inflation has had devastating effects on the coinage of some countries. Thus the plummeting value of the **mark** in Germany after the First World War led to the issue of aluminium coins worth 200 and 500 marks, while Austria in the same period was forced to issue bronze 100 and 200 **krone** coins and a cupro-nickel 1,000 krone. **Token coins** of local validity were issued in many parts of Germany, Westphalia producing a billion mark coin in gold-plated **German silver**. Coins and tokens, however, were soon swept away as inflation raced out of control and the prolific issues of paper money known as **Notgeld** became commonplace. Before inflation was brought under control the Reichsbank was forced to issue notes up to a value of 100 billion marks. Austria, Hungary, Poland and Czechoslovakia also issued notes with an astronomical face value during the early 1920s. Hungary suffered inflation after the Second World War and holds the record for the highest value of any note ever issued – a thousand million adopengos, equivalent to 20,000,000,000,000,000,000,000,000,000,000 pengös.

Ingot   Piece of precious metal, usually cast in a mould, and stamped with the weight and fineness. Though mainly used as a convenient method of storing bullion, ingots have been used as currency in many countries, notably Russia and Japan.

Interest-bearing notes   Paper money in the form of notes which guaranteed interest to the bearer date from the American War of Independence, when Connecticut issued notes promising 6% interest "at or before the end of one Year after the Expiration of the present War". The currency notes issued by the Confederacy during the Civil War also bore interest, to be paid on the cessation of hostilities, but as the Confederacy lost the war they were never redeemed. The *assignats* and *mandats* of the French Revolution also bore interest, but this was more than counterbalanced by their rapid depreciation. The only really successful interest-bearing notes were the American Federal issue of that name made during the Civil War. Other American notes in this category include the Compound Interest Treasury Notes (1863–4) and the $10 Refunding Certificates of 1879.

Invasion money   Paper money produced by belligerents for use by their troops in the invasion of enemy territory. The earliest examples date from 1914 and include German Reichsbank notes surcharged in Persian currency for use by Niedermayer's expeditionary force in its abortive invasion of central Iran, and British Treasury notes overprinted in Arabic for use in the Gallipoli landings of 1915. **Kronen** notes of the Austro-Hungarian Bank were overprinted in Italian by the fascist legionaries of Gabriele d'Annunzio when they seized the Adriatic seaport of Fiume. Germany overprinted notes following the invasion of Czechoslovakia and Poland in 1938–9 and Italy did likewise in Albania. Later the Germans produced special issues known as **Behelfszahlungsmittel** and **Verrechnungsscheine**. Special notes were also issued for the German invasion of the Ukraine, but the most prolific of the invasion issues was made by Japan for the various countries of Southeast Asia and the Pacific. The Americans and British prepared notes for use following the D-Day landings but these belong more properly under the heading of **Liberation Money**. Notes with values in M.A.L. (Military Authority Lire) were produced by the British for use in the Italian colonies in North Africa following their invasion in 1942–3.

Iron   Metal, chemical symbol *Fe* (from Latin *ferrum*), used as a primitive form of currency from classical times onward. Iron spits (*obeliskoi*) proceded the **obol** as the lowest unit of Greek coinage, a handful of six spits being worth a **drachma**. In China under the Sung, Ming and Ch'ing dynasties cast-iron pieces were used as a substitute for copper **cash**. Many of the **emergency token** issues of Germany during the First World War were struck in iron. Iron coins of 2, 5 or 10 **leva** were issued by Bulgaria in 1943. See also **Steel**.

Isabella   Spanish gold coin worth 5 douros, portraying Isabella II (1833–68).

Ishu Gin   Small rectangular coin, meaning literally "silver shu" (quarter **bu**) issued by Japan during the Shogunate up to 1860.

J

Jeon   Alternative spelling for **cheun**, the Korean unit of currency (100 = 1 won).

Jérôme d'or   Gold coin worth a **pistole** or 5 **talers** issued in the kingdom of Westphalia in 1810–13 during the reign of Jérôme Bonaparte. There was also a double jérôme.

Jeton   From French *jeter*, to throw. Alternative term for counter, and used originally on the chequerboard used by medieval accountants. Nuremberg was the most important centre for the production of medieval jetons, which were often issued in extensive series with portraits of contemporary rulers. At the present day the term is used loosely as a synonym for **token** and denotes pieces used in vending equipment, parking meters, telephones and urban transport systems in many European countries. Apart from security, the main advantage of such pieces is that they can be re-tariffed as charges increase, without any alteration in their design or composition, a method that is far cheaper than to alter costly equipment to take larger coins.

Joachimstaler   Name given to the **guldengroschen** struck by the Counts of Schlick from silver extracted from their mines at Joachimstal (Jachymov) in Bohemia in 1520. Though politically of no account, the Counts of Schlick owned the most prolific silver mines in Europe and their coins soon outpaced the output of the Elector of Saxony. The name was shortened to **taler** and came to apply to any large silver coin of similar appearance. The original placename was not immediately lost sight of, and many of the silver coins of the 16th century from other parts of Europe went under such names as joachimik (Poland), jefimok, jefimki (Russia), joachimico (Italy) or jacondale (France).

Joao   Portuguese gold coin first issued in 1722 under John V and derived from the Portuguese version of his name. Worth 6,400 **reis**, it rapidly became a popular trade coin all over Europe and circulated in America and eventually also as far afield as Australia. The joao was last minted in 1835.

Joe   West Indian term for the Portuguese **joao** and subsequently given to copies struck in Birmingham for circulation as trade coins in the Caribbean area and the American colonies.

Joey   Popular name for the silver **groat** or fourpenny piece which circulated in many of the British colonies during the 19th century.

Johanna   Portuguese gold coin worth 8 **escudos**, minted in 1723–32. The half johanna continued till 1750.

Jubilee coins   Coins issued to celebrate the silver (25th), golden (50th) or diamond (60th) jubilee of a ruler. Quite a number of the **talers** of the German principalities commemorated jubilees and this practice continued after the foundation of the German Empire in 1871. Among the later jubilee coins were the 20-**mark** gold coins of Anhalt (1896), silver 5-mark coin of Baden (1902), silver 3-mark coin of Hesse-Darmstadt (1917) and the 3-mark coin of Prussia (1913). Other countries which have issued jubilee coins include Austria (1908), Belgium (1976), Bulgaria (1912), Denmark (1903 and 1937), Hungary (1907), Monaco (1974), Netherlands and Netherlands Antilles (1973) and Sweden (1897). British Commonwealth countries issued coins for the Silver Jubilee of George V (1935) and almost 20 countries, from Australia to the Seychelles, issued coins for the Silver Jubilee of Queen Elizabeth in 1977.

Judenpfennig   German for Jewish penny, the name given to small copper tokens emanating mostly from Frankfurt am Main in the early 19th century and circulating among the Jewish communities of western Germany as small change.

Justo   Portuguese gold coin worth 2 **cruzados** issued under Joao II in 1485.

K

Ka-Kim   Engraved silver rings used as currency in Thailand till the late 18th century, produced in weights of 1, 2 and 4 **ticals**.

Kangaroo coins   Very rare gold pieces minted in Sydney, New South Wales, 1853, and depicting the national animal of Australia. The coins comprised quarter, half, 1 and 2 ounce pieces of fine gold. Many of the copper tokens issued by the Australian colinies in the mid-19th century also depicted a kangaroo on the obverse or reverse, and this was followed by the Commonwealth government as the reverse motif of the bronze penny and halfpenny of 1938–64.

Kapang (keping)   Copper coin of Sarawak, Malaya and Sumatro, 18th–19th centuries. Kepings of 1786 were the first coins to be struck by steam-press, at the Soho Mint of Boulton and Watt in Birmingham.

Kasu   Copper coin issued by the Indian state of Mysore from the mid-18th century, the name being the Hindi equivalent of the Chinese **cash**.

Kazbegi   Persian copper coins of the Safavid period (1502–1736), minted in denominations from half to 8 kazbegi.

Kina   Unit of currency in Papua New Guinea since 1975 (= 100 **toea**).

Kip   Unit of currency in Laos since 1949 (= 100 **att** or **centimes**).

Kipperzeit   German term meaning "the time of clipped coins", denoting the period during and after the Thirty Years War (1618–48) in which debased and clipped money was in circulation.

Kissi Penny   Name given to the primitive currency (consisting of iron rods) used by the Kissi tribe of West Africa in the 18th and 19th centuries.

Klippe   Rectangular or square pieces of metal bearing the impression of a coin. Coins of this type were first struck in Sweden in the 16th century and were subsequently produced in many of the German states, usually as a form of **emergency money**. The idea has been revived in recent years as a medium for striking commemorative pieces.

Knife money (also known as bill-hook, razor or sword money)   Cast bronze pieces, with an elongated blade and a ring at one end to facilitate stringing together in bunches, were used as currency in China from the 9th century B.C. onwards till the 19th century.

Koban   Elongated oval pieces of gold bearing **chop-marks** guaranteeing their weight and fineness were used as currency in Japan from 1600 till 1860. They were worth a tenth of an **oban**.

Kobo   Nigerian unit of currency introduced in 1973 (100 = 1 **naira**).

Kopek   Russian unit of currency, said to derive its name from the word *kop'io* (lance) from the reverse motif of St. George holding a lance. Introduced a part of the monetary reforms of 1534, it was the hundredth part of a **rouble**, and was thus the first decimal coin in the world. The half-kopek coin was known as a **denga**. Silver and latterly bronze were used for the kopeks of the tsarist period, brass or aluminium bronze being used in the Soviet period.

Kori   Silver coin of Kutch, worth 24 **dokda**, in circulation till 1947.

Korona (**koruna**), plural forms **koruny, koruncic**   Unit of currency in Hungary and equivalent to the Austrian **krone** (= 100 **filler**). The korona was superseded in Hungary by the **pengö** in 1926, but since 1918 has been the unit in Czechoslovakia (= 100 **haleru**).

Koula   Polynesian word for gold, denoting a gold coin worth £16, issued by Tonga, 1962. Half and quarter koula were also released.

Krajczar   Unit of currency in Hungary, being the Magyar equivalent of the German **kreuzer**, from 1868 to 1892. Copper half and 1 krajczar and silver 10- and 20-krajczar coins were issued.

Kran   Persian silver coin worth 20 **shahis** or 1,000 **dinars**, first struck in the reign of Fath Ali Shah (1826). Large silver coins worth 1, 2 and 5 krans were minted till 1926. Even larger pieces, allegedly worth 10 krans or 1 **toman**, are now believed to be either medals or patterns.

Kreditivsedlar   Swedish for "credit notes", and the name given to the first issue of paper money made in the Western world. Paper money of this type was the idea of Johan Palm-struch at Riga in 1652 but nine years elapsed before it was implemented by the Stockholm Bank. Originally redeemable in copper currency, the later issues were redeemable in silver **talers**, but were discontinued in 1665 when the Bank failed to make good its promise.

Kreuzer   Name given to many different coins of low value produced in the German-speaking areas of Europe, and derived from the double-lined cruciform motif (*Kreuz*) depicted on the earliest issues. The first kreuzer was minted by the Count of Goerz-Tirol at Merano in 1258 and under Meinhard II (1271–95) attained widespread popularity all over southern Germany and Austria as a trade coin. Such was its popularity that it was known as a "meinhard" for over a century. It became the unit of currency in Austria (till 1892) and the south German states (till 1872).

Krone   German word for crown, denoting the unit of currency in Austria (= 100 **heller**) from 1892 till 1926. The name was also given to the unit of currency adopted by Denmark in 1618 and originally denoting a large silver coin worth 1.5 speciedaler but later reduced in size and value. The krone was adopted as the unit by the **Scandinavian Monetary Union** in 1875 (= 100 öre). The different plural forms – **kroner**

(Denmark and Norway), **kronor** (Sweden) and **kronur** (Iceland) reflect the linguistic subtleties of the Scandinavian languages.

Kroon (plural **krooni**)   Unit of currency in the Baltic republic of Estonia from 1928 till 1940 (= 100 **senti**).

Krugerrand   Gold bullion piece issued by South Africa since 1967, containing a troy ounce of fine gold. Half, quarter and tenth Krugerrands were introduced in 1980. It derives its name from the effigy of Paul Kruger on the obverse.

Kuna   Russian word meaning a pine marten, subsequently denoting the pelt of this animal which was used as barter currency from the 11th century onwards and traded by the Tatars on part with the Arab **dirhem**. In medieval times it became a kind of money of account on the basis of 22 to the **grivna**. The kuna was revived as the unit of currency in the German puppet state of Croatia, 1942–4 (= 100 **banicas**).

Kurus   Unit of currency in Turkey since 1934 (100 = 1 **lira**).

Kuta   Unit of currency in Congo-Kinshasa (now Zaïre) since 1967. 100 **sengi** = 1 kuta; 100 kuta = 1 **zaïre**.

Kwacha   Unit of currency in Malawi since 1970 (= 100 **tambalas**).

Kwanza   Unit of currency in Angola since 1977 (= 100 **weis**).

Kwartnik   Small Polish silver coin worth half a **groszy**, first issued in the mid-14th century under Casimir the Great.

Kyat   Burmese unit of currency since 1952 (= 100 **pyas**).

L

Lari (laree, larin)   Originally a form of primitive currency consisting of drawn-silver bars or rods, circulating in Persia and Arabia, but latterly the unit of currency in the Maldive Islands. Bronze lari were first minted by Ralph Heaton of Birmingham in 1913, but since 1960 bronze or nickel-brass coins from 1 to 50 lari have been struck (100 = 1 **rupee**).

Latin Monetary Union (Union Latine)   Monetary convention between France, Switzerland, Italy and Belgium at the instigation of Napoleon III, designed to preserve the parity of their currencies. Greece joined the Union in 1868 and Spain in 1870, and in the last decades of the 19th century the Union's influence affected the size and weight of gold coins minted in other parts of the world, notably Latin America. The Union operated a **bimetallic** standard, of which the gold 20 **franc** piece and the silver 5 franc piece were the models. The coinage of the member countries was more or less standardised until 1914 when the Union collapsed. Napoleon III never quite realised his ambition of replacing **sterling** as the world trading standard, due to the strength of the British gold **sovereign** and the British practice of using 22 carat (.916) fine gold instead of the .900 fineness adopted by the Union. The Union's hopes of establishing an international currency were destroyed by the First World War.

Lats (plural lati)   Unit of currency in Latvia from 1918 till 1940 (= 100 **santimi**).

Laurel   British gold coin worth 20 **shillings**, minted in 1619–25 and deriving its name from the laureated effigy of King James I on the obverse.

Leather money   Pieces of leather embossed with an official device have been used as money on several occasions. Leather tokens were used by the beleaguered inhabitants of Faenza under siege by the Emperor Frederick II, and at Leiden during the siege of 1574 by the Spaniards. Several towns in Austria and Germany produced leather tokens during and after the First World War at **Notgeld**, notably Pössneck and Osterwieck. Leather tokens were circulated in the Isle of Man in the 15th and 16th centuries.

Legal tender   Term signifying coins or paper money offered in satisfaction of a liability or a debt and according with the proper legal requirements. In layman's language a legal tender coin is one which can be offered as payment and must be accepted in exchange for goods or services at the nominal value expressed on it. This gives rise to some curious anomalies. The British gold **sovereign** in the period 1965–70 was legal tender for 20 shillings, while it was actually illegal for any person, other than a registered dealer or collector, to possess more than two examples. Many precious metal coins of the present day have a legal tender value of 25 pence (e.g. the commemorative crowns of Britain and the Commonwealth), whereas their intrinsic value may amount to several pounds.

Legend   Inscription on a coin or medal.

Lek   Unit of currency in Albania since 1925 (= 100 **qindarka**).

Lempira   Dollar-sized silver coin introduced by Honduras in 1931, worth 100 **centavos**, as a result of the currency reform of 1926.

Leone   Unit of currency in Sierra Leone since 1964. 100 cents = 1 leone; 50 leones = 1 **golde**.

Leopard   Small gold coin issued under Edward III in 1344 and worth half a **florin** or 3 **shillings**. It derives its name from the heraldic leopard sejant on the obverse. Though English leopards are of the greatest rarity, a similar coin was minted from 1361 by Edward in his capacity as Duke of Aquitaine.

Lepton (plural **lepta**)   Greek unit of currency since 1831 (100 = 1 **drachma**), from the classical Greek word for a minute which also served as the name of a small copper coin in late classical times. In the Ionian Islands, under British administration, the lepton was worth a fifth of an **obol**, or a tenth of a British **penny**.

Leu (plural **lei**)   Unit of currency in Romania since 1867, worth 100 **bani** and modelled on the French **franc**. Gold coins from 12½ to 50 lei were struck in 1906 and silver 1, 2 and 5 lei from 1870, but due to inflation later issues were struck in cupro-nickel (1924), nickel-brass (1930), brass (1938–41), aluminium or aluminium-bronze (1948–51) and in nickel-steel since 1966. Silver 100,000 lei coins appeared during the inflationary period of 1946–7.

Lev (plural **leva**)   Bulgarian unit of currency, worth 100 **stotinki**, adopted in 1880 and, like the Romanian **leu**, modelled on the **franc** of the **Latin Monetary Union**. Struck in virtually every coinage alloy from gold or iron at various times, it reflects the violent fluctuations in the economy over the past century.

Li   Smallest unit of currency in Manchukuo, 1932–45. Copper 5 li or ½ fen were issued in 1933–9.

Liang   Chinese equivalent of the ounce, a silver unit of weight which later became the **tael**.

Liard   Originally a small silver coin worth 3 **deniers**, first minted under Louis XI in the mid-15th century, it was reduced to a copper coin in 1649. In this form it continued to be struck till 1786 but was not actually demonetised till 1845.

Liberation money   Paper money prepared for use in parts of Europe and Asia, formerly under Axis occupation. The notes produced by the Allies for use in France after D-Day (1944) were originally inscribed *Emis en France* (issued in France) and bore the French tricolour, but General de Gaulle took exception to these features. Later issues were merely inscribed "France" and omitted the flag. Liberation currency was also produced for use in Belgium and the Netherlands, but the latter objected to the designs and they were soon withdrawn. Indian notes were overprinted for use in Burma when that country was liberated from the Japanese. Various Japanese occupation and Chinese bank notes were overprinted for use in Hong Kong when it was liberated in 1945.

Libra   Roman word for **pound**, used as the name of a Peruvian gold coin of 1898. The French **livre**, the Italian and Turkish **lira** and the English £ notation for a **pound** all stem from the Roman libra.

Licente   Lesotho equivalent of the South African **rand**. 100 cents = 1 licente; 100 licente = **1 maloti**.

Ligature   From Latin *ligatus* – bound. Term denoting the linking of two letters in a legend, e.g. Æ, Ν (AU) and Œ.

Lilangeni   Unit of currency in Swaziland since 1974 (= 100 **cents**). A gold piece of this name was issued in 1968 with a nominal value of 25 **luhlanga**.

Lira (plural **lire**)   Italian unit of currency derived from the Roman **libra** and first used as a coinage value by Venice in 1472. Hitherto it had served as **money of account**, as a means of expressing **denarii**. The Venetian lira was intended as the Italian counterpart to the Tirolese **guldengroschen** but was somewhat lighter. Because the first lira portrayed the Doge, Nicolò Tron, it was unpopular with the Venetians. Galeazzo Maria Sforza also produced portrait lire, but these were more substantial and later became known as the **testone**. Lire were eventually minted in a number of Italian states and became the unit for the unified kingdom of Italy in 1862 (= 100 **centesimi**). Subsequently it was adopted by San Marino (1898) and the Vatican (1929) and spread to Turkey in 1933 (= 100 **piastres** or **kurus**) and Israel (1948). The Israeli pound or lira (plural **lirot**) was originally worth 1,000 **pruta** but since 1963 has been retariffed at 100 **agorot**.

Lis   Name given to French coins in gold (*lis d'or*) and silver (*lis d'argent*), authorised by Louis XIV in 1655, though rare proofs dated 1653 exist. The name is derived from the lilies depicted on the reverse.

Litas (plural **litu** or **litai**)   Unit of currency in Lithuania from 1918 to 1940 (= 100 **centas**). Silver coins in denominations of 1, 2, 5 and 10 litai were issued between 1925 and 1938.

Litra   Unit of weight in Sicily in the 4th century B.C., the counterpart of the Roman **libra**. Gold coins worth 50 (*pentekontalitrae*) and 100 (*hekatonlitrae*) were minted at Syracuse, while silver or bronze litrae were worth a tenth of a Corinthian **stater**.

Livre   French word for **pound**, from the Latin **libra**, serving as the basis of weights and currency from the time of Charlemagne in the 9th century. The Carolingian Empire instituted the £sd system, the livre being worth 20 **sols** or **sous**, or 240 **denarii** or **deniers**. In the Middle Ages the value of the livre fluctuated from one area to another, but gradually the *livre tournois* won ascendancy over the *livre parisis* (the latter tariffed at the ratio of 4 to 5 of the former). In the late 14th century a gold coin worth a livre tournois was introduced and rapidly won popularity as the *franc à cheval*, so that the words livre and **franc** became synonymous. Later, however, it was used mainly as money of account, fluctuating against the **écu** in the 18th century according to the prevailing state of the French economy. A silver livre worth 20 **sols** was struck in 1720 for the ill-fated Compagnie des Indes founded by John Law.

Long Cross Penny   Type of silver penny introduced by Henry III in 1247 and deriving its name from the reverse which bore a cross whose arms extended right to the edge to help safeguard the coins against **clipping**. This remained the style of the silver penny, its fractions and multiples till the reign of Henry VIII, and vestiges of the long cross theme can be seen in the silver coins throughout the remaining years of the Tudor period.

Louis d'argent   Crown-sized silver coin, originally known as the **écu** blanc, introduced in 1641 in the reign of Louis XIII of France. Worth 60 **sols**, it was issued also in fractions (half, quarter and twelfth). The louis d'argent was the principal silver coin till the outbreak of the Revolution in 1789.

Louis d'or   French gold coin adopted in 1640 and deriving its name from Louis XIII whose profile appeared on the obverse. The gold louis was worth 10 **livres** and it was also struck in multiples of 2, 4, 6, 8 and 10 louis, the lastnamed being the highest denomination of any French coin ever issued. Like the silver louis, it continued until 1789.

Luhlanga   Unit of currency in Swaziland, 1968. 100 cents = 1 luhlanga; 25 luhlanga = 1 **lilangeni**.

Lusshebourne   English word for base **pennies** of inferior silver, said to have emanated from Luxembourg, from which the name derived. These coins were first minted under John the Blind who adopted the curious spelling of his name EIWANES in the hope that illiterate English merchants might confuse it with EDWARDVS and thus be accepted as coin issued in the name of King Edward III. Lusshebournes were also struck by Robert of Bethune, William I of Namur and the bishops of Toul in the mid-14th century.

Lweis   Unit of currency in Angola since 1977 (100 lweis = 1 **kwanza**).

M

Mace English term for the Chinese *ch'ien* denoting a tenth of a silver **tael** and found in the inscription on Chinese imperial silver **dollars** and half-dollars – 7 mace 2 **candareens** and 3 mace 6 candareens respectively.

Macuta (plural **licuta**) Copper coin worth 50 **reis** used as money in the Portuguese colonies in Africa since 1762. Multiple licuta were struck in silver. See also **Kuta.**

Magdalon d'or Gold **florin** produced at Aix-en-Provence and Tarascon from 1476 to 1481 and deriving its name from the effigy of Mary Magdalene on the obverse.

Magnimat Trade name used by VDM (*Verein Deutscher Metallwerke*) for a high-security alloy containing copper, nickel and magnetised steel. First used for the 5 deutschmark coin of 1975, it has since been adopted for other high-value coins in Germany and other countries. A golden lustre variant of magnimat is known as **virenium.**

Mandat Shortened form of *mandat territorial* (territorial money order) adopted by the French Directory in 1795. These orders or land warrants constituted a mortgage on all the lands in the French Republic and were intended to supersede the **assignats** which had become virtually worthless. They were no more successful and on the day of their issue were discounted by 82%. They lasted only six months and were redeemed by the State in 1796 at a 70th of their face value in coin.

Mandaten Treasury notes with values in **rixdalers**, issued by the Boer republics of South Africa in the mid-19th century.

Manilla   Copper, bronze or brass rings, sometimes shaped like horseshoes and sometimes open, with flattened terminals, used as currency in West Africa until recent years. In Nigeria, where they were widely used until 1948, they circulated at values between 2 and 6 **pence**.

Marabotin   Moorish gold **dinar** of the El Murabitin dynasty, minted in southern Spain.

Maravedi   Originally a gold coin struck in Castile in the early Middle Ages in imitation of Arab **dinars**, it became the copper unit of currency under Ferdinand and Isabella, 375 being worth one gold **excelente**. Multiples of 2, 4, 6 and 8 maravedis survived until the decimal system was adopted in 1867–8.

Marengo   French 20-**franc** gold coin struck in 1801 to commemorate the victory of that name the previous year.

Maria Theresa taler   Austrian silver coin with the effigy of the Empress Maria Theresa on the obverse and the imperial arms on the reverse. Talers of this type dated 1780 (the year of the death of the empress) were widely used as trade coins in the Levant, the Near and Middle East and northeast Africa. Although the taler was demonetised in Austria in 1854, these coins continued to be struck at the Vienna Mint, and have also been copied down to the present by the Royal Mint (London) and mints in Rome, Paris, Brussels, Bombay and Birmingham for circulation in the Arab countries and Ethiopia.

Mariengroschen   Silver coin deriving its name from the portrait of the Virgin Mary depicted on the obverse. First minted at Goslar in 1505 it became widely popular in many parts of Germany till the mid-19th century. The mariengroschen was worth 8 **pfennigs** and tariffed at 36 to the **taler**.

Mark   Originally a unit of weight in the Carolingian Empire (= 8 ounces or half a Carolingian pound), it came to signify a unit which varied in weight from one part of Germany to another. Eventually the Cologne fine mark was taken as the standard bullion measure for the entire German-speaking area and many of the silver coins of the 17th–19th centuries indicate in their inscriptions how many of them were tariffed to the Cologne mark. The mark of 100 pfennigs was adopted as the unit of currency in the German Empire in 1875, and this has continued to the present day, sometimes known as the reichsmark (till 1945), or the deutschmark of West Germany (since 1950), with the notation RM or DM respectively. In the German Democratic Republic, the notation MDN (*Mark der Deutsche Notenbank*) appeared on coins and banknotes of the 1960s. The mark has also, at one time or another, been the unit of currency in Denmark, Estonia, Livonia, Norway and Sweden.

Markka (plural **Markkaa**)   Unit of currency in Finland since 1860, during the period of the Russian grand-duchy in the 19th century (= 100 **pennia**). Gold 20 and 10 markkaa coins were struck during the tsarist period, as well as silver 1 and 2 markkaa coins. The markka was introduced by J.V Snellman, Minister of Finance in the grand-duchy, and his portrait appears on the obverse of the 1,000 markkaa coins issued in 1960 to celebrate the centenary of the currency reform.

Masson   Silver coin of Lorraine and Bar, worth 20 **sous** 10 **deniers**, issued in 1728.

Matapan   Silver coin introduced by Enrico Dandolo, Doge of Venice, 1192, Worth 12 **denari** or 26 **piccoli**, it was the first large silver coin of the **grosso** type minted anywhere in Italy.

Matoña   Copper coin of Ethiopia, 1889–1931 (100 = 1 **talari**).

Matrix   Secondary die for a coin or medal, produced from the master die by means of an intermediary punch. In this way dies can be duplicated from the original cut on the reducing machine.

Mattier (**Matier, Matthier**)   **Groschen** deriving its name from the portrait of St. Matthew, and first minted early in the 15th century for use in the bishopric of Hildesheim. These groschen later spread to Goslar and by the 17th century were popular in many parts of Germany. The name was mostly used as a colloquialism, but actually appears on coins of Brunswick and Brandenburg in the 17th and 18th centuries, the name being rendered as "Matier" or "Mattier".

Maundy money   Set of small silver coins, in denominations of 1, 2, 3 and 4 pence, distributed by the reigning monarch to the poor and needy on Maundy Thursday. This custom dates back to the Middle Ages, but in its present form it dates from 1666 when the custom of distributing pence to as many men and women as the years in the monarch's age was adopted. So long as silver coins of these denominations were produced for general circulation no special minting was required, but from the reign of George II (1727–60) the coins tended increasingly to be restricted to the Maundy minting. Coins were minted sporadically till 1816 but since that date they have appeared annually. Sterling silver was used till 1922 when .500 fine silver was substituted, but when the circulating coinage changed to cupro-nickel in 1947 the use of sterling silver for Maundy coins was resumed. Since 1971 the coins have denoted decimal pence, but the designs remained unchanged. For centuries the Maundy ceremony took place in Westminster Abbey but since 1955 other venues have been used in alternate years.

Mazuna   Bronze coin of Morocco till 1922. 50 mazunas = 1 **dirhem**.

Medal   English term derived from French *medaille* and Italian *medaglia* from the Latin *metallum* and signifying a piece of metal bearing devices and legends, commemorating an event or person, or given as an award. Though often coinlike in appearance, medals have no monetary significance. Military medals have their origins in biblical times but the great majority date from the 16th and 17th centuries when they were conferred on officers for outstanding exploits. The first English medal granted to all ranks participating in a campaign was the Dunbar Medal (1651) but this did not become a regular custom till the Battle of Waterloo (1815). General service medals for the Army and Navy were instituted in 1847 and made retrospective right back to the beginning of the Napoleonic Wars, bars or clasps being attached to the ribbon to denote specific engagements and campaigns. This system has since spread to every country. At the same time the system of gallantry awards has been greatly developed and ranges from simple medals worn on ribbons on the breast, to elaborate stars and badges, collar pendants and other decorations. Commemorative medals can trace their origins from Roman imperial times, but in their present form date from the Italian Renaissance when there was a vogue for large-diameter cast bronze medals. Die-struck medals became more fashionable in France and Germany in the 16th century and gradually spread to other countries. By the late 17th century the medal was also being used as a propaganda medium, a custom which survived as late as the First World War. Commemorative medals declined in popularity after 1920 but revived in the 1960s, mainly in precious metals and celebrating events and personalities of international importance. Though the majority of medals are circular, quite a few are square, rectangular or octagonal and the term **plaque** or **plaquette** is then more properly used.

Medalet   A small medal, generally 2.5 cm or less in diameter.

Medallion   Synonym for medal, but usually confined to those with a diameter of 5 cm or more.

Meinhard   Nickname for the **kreuzer**, alluding to Meinhard II (1271–95) in whose reign it first received widespread popularity in southern Germany and Austria.

Merk   Scottish unit of weight and money of account, worth two-thirds of a **pound**. Half and quarter merk coins were introduced in 1572 and the two-merks or thistle **dollar** and the merk followed in 1578–9. The balance half and quarter merks appeared in 1591, followed by new thistle merks and subdivisions (half, quarter and eighth) in 1601. Half, one, two and four merk silver coins were also minted in the reign of Charles II (1664–75).

Mil   From Latin *mille*, thousand. Unit of currency in Cyprus, Malta and Palestine (1,000 = £1).

Milan d'or   Gold coin worth 20 **dinars** issued in Serbia in 1882 and deriving its name from the effigy of King Milan I on the obverse.

Miliarense (Miliaresia, miliarensium)   Silver coin adopted by Constantine the Great in the early 4th century A.D. and mainly associated with the reigns of his successors, Constans and Constantius. Later it was a unit of currency under the Byzantine Empire (1,000 = 1 Byzantine **pound**).

Military Payment Certificates   Paper money used by American servicemen for purchases at the post exchange or for circulation within the limits of military base, and intended to thwart the activities of speculators and black marketeers.

Military Payment Warrants   Form of paper money dating from the 17th century, used as a convenient method of arranging the pay for soldiers on campaigns and expeditions. They were issued by the Command Paymaster to the commanders of regiments who used them to draw coined money from local banks.

Millième   French variant of mil, the thousandth part of a pound in Egypt, Libya and the Sudan.

Millime   Tunisian unit of currency since 1960 (1,000 = 1 **dinar**).

Milling   Process denoting the mechanical production of coins, as opposed to the handmade technique implied in **hammering**. It alludes to the use of watermills to drive the machinery of the screw presses developed in the 16th century. Milled coins were pioneered in France although credit for the invention of the rolling mill goes to an Augsburg engineer named Max Schwab. This enabled **bullion** to be rolled out into strips of uniform thickness, from which coin blanks could be cut. A mechanised mint was established at the Moulin des Etuves (mill of the baths) on the Seine at the tip of the Ile du Palais in 1551 and milled coins for general circulation were produced from 1552, but production declined in face of opposition from the Cour des Monnaies and the hammermen. Eloi Mestrel, a Huguenot refugee, brought the milling process to England but after an initial period

(1561–72) Mestrel was dismissed and it was not until 1662 that production of milled coinage was resumed. The characteristic evenness of thickness and regularity of diameter in milled coins permitted the use of a security edge, hence the popular but erroneous use of the term "milling" to signify **graining** or **reeding**.

Milreis   Portuguese unit of currency worth 1,000 **reis**, issued as a crown-sized silver coin in 1836–45 and 1898–1910. It was also used in Brazil till 1942, coins of 1, 2 or 4 milreis being struck from 1851 onwards.

Mina   Unit of weight in ancient Greece, worth 100 **drachmae** or a sixtieth of a **talent**. It was used as money of account and never as an actual coin.

Minimus   Latin word for smallest. Name given to the very tiny bronze coins issued by the Belgic and Celtic tribes of Britain immediately before the Roman occupation, and later applied also to the even smaller coins of the Roman Empire in the 3rd century A.D.

Mining taler   Term denoting the **talers** and multiple talers produced by many German principalities in the 15th–18th centuries as a convenient way of handling the silver produced by their mines. Many of these handsome large-diameter pieces bore references to the source of the metal or depicted aspects of the mining and refining of silver.

Mint   The place in which coins and medals are produced. Mint condition is a term sometimes used to denote pieces in an uncirculated state.

Mint mark   A device appearing on a coin to denote the place of minting. Such symbols are known from classical times, the *tetradrachms* of the 4th century B.C. being known with tiny marks such as the rose (Rhodes), helmet (Mesembria) or bee (Ephesus). Athenian coins have been recorded with up to 40 different marks, denoting the individual workshops from which the emanated. Early in the 4th century A.D. the Romans adopted this system to identify coins struck in provincial mints, often using letters of the alphabet. This system continued in the Middle Ages and survives to this day.

Thus British pennies struck at Kings Norton or the Heaton mint, Birmingham, bear mint-marks KN or H in the **exergue**. Countries having more than one mint also use this system; American coins may be found with the mint marks S (San Francisco), D (Dahlonega) or P (Philadelphia). German coins since 1875 may be found with the letters A (Berlin), B (Hanover), C (Frankfurt), D (Munich), E (Dresden), F (Stuttgart), G (Karlsruhe), H (Darmstadt) or J (Hamburg). After moneyers' names or initials ceased to appear on English coins in the reign of Edward I (1272–1307), symbols were adopted to denote provincial mints. From 1351 onwards, however, these symbols, derived from contemporary heraldic practice, were used to denote periods between trials of the **pyx**, and thus assist the proper chronological sequence of coins, in an era prior to the adoption of dating. These mint marks continued into the 17th century, but gradually died out as the use of dates became more widespread.

See also **Countermark, Privy Mark.**

Mionnet Scale   Scale of 19 diameters covering all sizes of coins belonging to the classical period, devised by the French numismatist Théodore-Edmé Mionnet (1770–1842) during the compilation of his 15-volume catalogue of the numismatic collection in the Bibliothèque Nationale in Paris.

Mirror finish   Term denoting the highly polished surface of proof coins.

Model Coin   Tiny pieces of metal, either reproducing the designs of existing coins (used as play money by children) or, more specifically, denoting patterns produced by Joseph Moore and Hyam Hyams in their attempts to promote an improved subsidiary coinage in 19th century Britain. These small coins were struck in bronze with a brass or silver centre and were designed to reduce the size of the existing cumbersome range of pence, halfpence and farthings.

Mohar   Silver or gold coins of Nepal, 1881–1937 worth 16 **dak** or 32 **paise.**

Mohur   Indian gold coin worth 15 **rupees,** minted by Bikanir, Gwalior, Hyderabad, Kutch and Rajkot until 1937.

Moidore   Corruption of the Portuguese *moeda de ouro* (money of gold) denoting the gold 500 **reis** (1575) or the 4 **cruzado** (1663–1722).

Mon (Meung)   Japanese copper coin, superseded by the **sen** in the decimal system adopted in 1870, on the ratio of 100 mon to 1 sen.

Moneta Patriottica   Italian for "patriotic money", inscribed on paper money issued by the defenders of Venice in 1848, during the siege of the city by the Austrians.

Money of Account   Term signifying a unit of value used in business transactions but not existing in the form of actual coin or paper money. Thus the **sestertius** and **libra** served as money of account in Roman times, as the **mina** and **talent** did in the ancient Greek world. At various times the £sd system of medieval Italy, later adopted in England, denoted money of account in **lire** (**pounds**) and **soldi** or **solidi** (**shillings**) in relation to **denari** or **denarii** (**pence**) when, in fact, only the latter existed as actual coins. From 1816 **guineas** were used in Britain as money of account to denote 21 **shillings** (£1.05), just as **livres** were used in France, or **marks** in medieval Germany.

Money order   Certificate for a specified amount of money, which may be transmitted by post and encashed at a money order office or post office. This system was pioneered by Britain and the United States in the mid-19th century and is now virtually worldwide. The term is now confined to certificates above a certain value, the terms **postal order** or **postal note** being used for similar certificates covering small amounts.

Mongo (mung)   Copper coin of Mongolia, struck in aluminium since 1970. 100 mongo = 1 **tugrik**.

Mortuary Coins and Medals   Coins and medals struck by a monarch to commemorate his predecessor. This custom was widespread in classical times, deriving from the Greek coins portraying the deified Alexander the Great and reaching its peak in Imperial Rome.

Mouton d'or   French for "golden sheep" and denoting a gold coin depicting the Lamb of God, issued by France in the 14th and 15th centuries. The value of these coins varied from 20 to 25 **sous**.

Mule   Coin, token or medal whose obverse is not matched with its official or regular reverse. Mules are known from Imperial Roman times, with the obverse die referring to an emperor and the reverse referring to a predecessor or another member of the imperial family. Accidental mules in recent years have resulted from the mixing of **dies** at mints where coins of several countries are struck. This gives rise to such famous mules as the Coronation Anniversary crowns with Ascension and Isle of Man dies, or 2 cent coins with Bahamas and New Zealand dies. Isle of Man reverse dies were deliberately muled with British obverses to produce copper coins with dates after 1839 when Manx coinage was discontinued, and restrikes of rare American coins have been detected in which the dated die has been paired with the wrong reverse die, e.g. the 1860 restrike of the rare 1804 large cent.

Mun (mung)   Korean variant of the Japanese **mon**. Copper 5 and 10 mun coins were issued in 1888.

Mute   **Anepigraphic** coin, identifiable only by the devices struck on it.

N

Nail mark Small indentation on ancient coins. The earliest coins of Asia Minor developed from the **electrum dumps** which merchants marked with a broken nail as their personal guarantee of value, the ancient counterpart of the **chop-mark** used in China and Japan.

Naira Unit of currency in Nigeria since 1973 (= 100 kobo).

Nami Sen Japanese for "wave money", signifying four-**mon** coins of the 18th century which had a wavy-line motif on the reverse.

Napoleon Popular name for the French 20-**franc** gold coin, first minted in 1803 and last produced in 1914. Production reached its peak in the reign of Napleon III (1852–70), some 242 million being minted, or more than the total output of **sovereigns** in the entire reign of Queen Victoria (1837–1901).

Naya Paisa (new paisa) Indian decimal unit (100 = 1 **rupee**) introduced 1957. The adjective naya was dropped in 1964.

Negotiepenning Dutch trade coin struck in gold from 1848 till the adoption of the gold standard in 1875. Though not given an actual value, it bore on the reverse its weight and fineness. Half and double negotiepennings were also minted.

Ngultrum Bhutanese name for the **rupee** (= 100 **chetrum**).

Ngwee Zambian unit of currency since 1968 (100 = 1 kwacha).

Nicked coin   Coin bearing a tiny cut or nick in its edge. Silver coins were tested by this method, especially in the reign of Henry I (1100–35) when so many base silver pennies were in circulation. Eventually people refused to accept these nicked coins – a problem which was only overcome when the state decreed that all coins should have a nick in them.

Nickel   Metallic element (chemical symbol Ni). This hard white metal is relatively resistant to tarnish and is ideally suited to coinage, especially in the 20th century as a cheap substitute for silver. When the American silver half dime was replaced by a nickel 5 cent coin in 1866 the latter soon acquired the nickname "nickel" by which it is known to this day, even though other coins formerly struck in silver are now minted in an alloy of copper and nickel also. Although best known as a silver substitute it was widely used in Jamaica (1869–1969) for halfpence and pennies and in British West Africa for the tiny 1/10th pennies (1908–57). Pure nickel is used for French francs and German marks, but usually it is alloyed with copper or zinc to produce cupro-nickel or nickel brass.

Noble   English coin introduced by Edward III in 1344 as a successor to the short-lived **florin** or double **leopard** which had been overvalued in relation to its weight. The noble was tariffed at 80 **pence**, half a **mark** or a third of a **pound**. Half- and quarter-nobles were also minted. The obverse depicted the king standing in a ship, allegedly a reference to the naval victory of the English over the French at Sluys. The last nobles appeared in the reign of Henry VIII (1526), when a new coin, the **george noble** (with reverse of St. George and the Dragon) was briefly introduced as part of a plan to revalue the gold coinage. This coin, worth 6s 8d, took the place of the **angel** which was then increased in value from 6s 8d to 7s 4d.

Nomisma   Greek word for money, but applied specifically to a gold coin of the Byzantine Empire, originally on par with the **solidus** but later devalued and struck in **electrum**, silver and even copper.

Nonsunt   Groat worth 12 pence minted in Scotland in the names of Mary Queen of Scots and her first husband, Francis II of France. It takes it name from the Latin legend *Iam non sunt duo sed una caro* (Now we are not two, but one flesh).

Notaphily   Hybrid word from Latin *nota* (note) and Greek *philos* (love), coined about 1970 to denote the branch of numismatics devoted to the study of paper money.

Notgeld   German word meaning emergency money, applied to the **tokens**, in metals, wood and even ceramic materials, issued during the First World War when coinage disappeared from circulation. These tokens were soon superseded by low-denomination paper money issued by shops and businessmen in denominations from 10 to 50 **pfennigs** and known as *kleine Notgeld* (small emergency money). These notes were prohibited in September 1922 but by that time some 50,000 varieties are thought to have been issued. Inflation raced out of control and the state permitted a second issue of local notes, known as large Notgeld since the denominations were in thousands or even millions of **marks**. Some 3,600 types appeared late in 1922 and over 60,000 in 1923 alone. They quickly ceased to have any real value, but were immensely popular with collectors, and it is evident from the fact that they were often published in sets that local authorities regarded Notgeld as a tourist medium, rather like picture postcards. These colourful and quaint mementoes of the German hyper-inflation ceased in 1924 when the currency was reformed.

Numismatics   The study of coins, medals and other related fields, a term derived from the Latin *numisma* and Greek *nomisma* (money).

Nummion (nummium, plural nummia)   Unit of weight in the Byzantine Empire, used in the denominations of bronze coins, the smallest of which was worth 2 nummia. Coins were minted at Alexandra worth 3, 6, 12 and 33 nummia, while Thessalonica produced coins worth 2, 3, 4, 5, 8 and 16 nummia, and Carthage and Constantinople minted 10, 20, 30 and 40 nummia coins.

Nummus   Simply the Latin word for a coin, but applied in the plural as a generic term to the very tiny copper pieces of the 5th century. It has been estimated that at least 7,200 nummi equalled the **solidus,** by that time no more than **money of account,** and they reflected the severe deflation which accompanied the fall of the Roman Empire in the west.

O

Oban   Japanese gold coin consisting an elongated oval disc, issued between the late 16th century and the beginning of the Meiji era (1868). The oban was worth 10 **rio** in gold or 20,000 **mon** in copper.

Obol (obolos, plural **oboloi)**   Smallest unit of currency in ancient Greece, tariffed at 6 to the **drachma**. The name is derived from *obeliskos*, a dart or spit, and alludes to the origin of this denomination as a kind of barter currency. The half obol was known as the hemiobol while larger denominations were the diobol, trihemiobol, triobol and tetrobol. The term was also used in the Middle Ages in Germany, Hungary and France to denote small coinage. The obol was also the unit of currency in the Ionian Islands under British administration (1814–64).

Obsidional Money   From Latin *obsidium*, siege. Term for **emergency money** produced by the defenders of besieged towns and cities. These usually took the form of pieces of silver plate, commandeered for the purpose, crudely marked with an official device and the value. Examples of this type date from the siege of Pavia in 1524 and include the siege coins of Rome (1527), Vienna (1529), Jülich (1543, 1610 and 1621), Frankenthal (1623), Magdeburg (1629), Greifswald (1631), Breisach (1633) and Minden (1634), the latter examples occurring during the Thirty Years War. The English Civil War also produced a fine crop of siege coinage from Carlisle (1644–5), Newark (1645–6), Pontefract (1648–9) and Scarborough (1644–5). From the struggle of the Netherlands against Spanish rule in the 16th century came the siege money of Alkmaar (1573), Middelburg (1574), Amsterdam (1578), Deventer (1578), Maastricht (1579) and Brussels (1580), as well as the famous leather tokens of Leiden (1572–3). Siege coins are known from towns besieged during the War of the Austrian Succession: Ulm (1704), Lille (1708), Tournai (1709), Aire (1711) and Landau (1713), while the war between Sweden and Russia yielded siege money from Stralsund (1713). Paper money was issued in Venice during the siege by Austria in 1848 and by Mafeking in 1900 during the Boer War.

Obverse   The "heads" side of a coin or medal, generally bearing the effigy of the head of state or an allegorical figure (e.g. Liberty – Argentina, Unites States; Helvetia – Switzerland, or la Semeuse – France).

Occupation money   Paper money and, more rarely, coins, issued by belligerents for use in territory under their occupation. In this category come the issues made by the Japanese for use in the areas of China, Southeast Asia and the Pacific under their occupation (1931–45), by Italy for use in Greece and the Ionian Islands and also prepared but not issued in Egypt and the Sudan, by Germany in many parts of Europe (1939–44), by Britain for use in the Faeroes (1940–5) and by the Allies for use in Austria and Germany (1945). See also **Invasion** and **Liberation Money**.

Octadrachm   Silver coin worth 8 **drachmae** first issued by Alexander I of Macedonia in the late 5th century B.C. and subsequently by the Phoenician city of Sidon. Gold octadrachms were minted under the Ptolemies in Egypt in the 3rd century B.C.

Octobol   Largest multiple of the **obol**, struck in silver in Chalcis and Histaia in the 3rd century B.C.

Oncia   Italian unit of weight, from Latin *uncia*, ounce, used in Florence in the Middle Ages for the 20th part of a **florin**. The oncia was also a silver coin of Malta (= 30 **tari**) and a gold coin of Sicily in the 18th century of the same value.

Order   From Latin *ordo*, an association of a limited number of persons bound by certain vows and obligations and subjected to certain rules. From the original monastic sense developed the orders of chivalry in the Middle Ages –

the Teutonic Knights, the Knights Templar, the Hospitallers of Jerusalem, Rhodes and Malta. The religious orders of chivalry developed into temporal orders in the Middle Ages and from the 14th century onwards royal knighthoods, aimed at strengthening the prestige of the monarch, were established in many European countries. The growth of republicanism at the end of the 18th century led to more democratic orders of merit, and the development of classes or grades in many of the existing orders. Alongside these orders arose the military orders, such as the Dutch *Willemsorden* (1815) and the British Distinguished Service Order (1886). In the 20th century the range of orders has been widened to include orders for science and the arts, and socialists orders of state. Other categories include personal royal orders such as the Royal Victorian Order, and female orders, such as the motherhood orders of Eastern Europe and the Greek Order for Good Deeds (1948). Numismatically these orders are of interest on account of their insignia which may consist of the star or breast badge, the collar, pectoral cross, medal (usually confined to lower classes of the order) and special ornaments such as oak leaves, palms, stars, crossed swords or crowns.

Ore (öre, øre)   Scandinavian unit of currency, derived from the Roman *aureus*. Originally a unit of weight used during the Middle Ages, worth an eighth of a **mark**, it later became **money of account** varying in value from 24 to 27 **pennings**. It first appeared as a coin in 1522 when **billon** ore were struck under Gustavus Vasa and tariffed at 2 **örtugar** or 4 **fyrkar**. In the 17th century copper and silver ore were minted as subdivisions of the **riksdaler**, and from 1776 till 1855 Sweden produced ore as half **skilling** coins. The **Scandinavian Monetary Union** (1873) adopted the ore as the hundredth part of the **krona**.

Ort   Polish and Prussian silver coin worth 18 **groschen**, 8 **gutegroschen** or quarter *taler*, derived from the Polish word for quarter.

Örtug (plural örtugar)   Smallest unit in Scandinavian **money of account**, originally a third of an **öre**. It first appeared as a coin in the Swedish province of Gotland in

1320, but was adopted generally by Gustavus Vasa in 1522 as the half-öre coin and continued till the end of the 16th century.

Overdate   One or more digits in a date altered by superimposing another figure. Alterations of this kind, by means of small hand punches, were made to dated dies so that they could be used in years other than that of the original manufacture. Coins with overdates invariably show traces of the original digit. Many 18th century British and 19th century American coins exhibit overdates.

Overstrike   Coin, token or medal produced by using a previously struck piece as a flan. The Bank of England dollar of 1804 was overstruck on Spanish pieces of eight, and examples showing traces of the original coins are worth a good premium.

P

Pa'anga　　Tongan unit of currency since 1967 (= 100 seniti). 100 pa'anga = 1 **hau**.

Paduan　　Name given to imitations of medals and bogus coins produced in Italy in the 16th century, and deriving from the city of Padua where forgeries of bronze sculpture were produced for the antique market.

Pagoda　　Gold coin struck in various parts of southern India in the early Middle Ages, but revived by the European powers in the 17th and 18th centuries for circulation in the territories under their control and generally worth 42 **fanams**. Subdivisions were also struck in silver. The name derives from the pagoda or temple featured on many of these coins. Gold pagodas continued to circulate in Travancore till 1924.

Pahlevi　　Gold coin struck in Iran from 1928 till 1961 and deriving its name from the reigning dynasty. Half, 2 and 5 pahlevis were also minted in the same period.

Pai　　see **Pie**

Paisa (baisa, baiza, besa, beza).　　Unit of currency in India (plural **paise**) from the adoption of the decimal system in 1957 (100 paise = 1 **rupee**). A similar system was adopted by Pakistan in 1961. Bronze, brass or copper paise were also circulated in many of the former Indian principalities, such as Bahawalpur (1924–5), Dungarpur (1944). Bundi had a quarter paisa (1916–29).

Palladium　　Precious metal of the platinum group, chemical symbol Pd, used for the quarter, half and 1 **hau** coins of Tonga, 1967.

Panama Pill   Nickname given to the 2½ **centesimo** coin issued by Panama in 1904 – the smallest silver coin of modern times.

Pano   Copper coin circulating in the Portuguese African territories, worth 5 **reis** or a tenth of a **macuta**.

Paolo   Papal coin worth 10 **baiocchi** or a tenth of a Roman **scudo**.

Papetto   Italian for "little Pope", signifying the papal 20 **baiocchi** silver coin of 1831–66.

Para (plural **paras** or **parades**)   Small Turkish coin, originally in silver but later in bronze or cupro-nickel, worth a fortieth of a **piastre**.

Pardao   Silver coin circulating in Portuguese India, 18th–19th centuries.

Parisis d'or   French gold coin introduced by Philippe VI in 1329, struck in pure (24 carat) gold and worth one **livre** parisis or Parisian pound.

Pataca   Unit of currency in the Portuguese colony of Macau (= 100 **avos**).

Patina   Oxidation forming on the surface of metallic objects. So far as coins and medals are concerned this applies mainly to silver, brass, bronze and copper pieces which may acquire oxidation from the atmosphere, or spectacular patination from salts in the ground in which they have been buried. In extreme forms patina leads to verdigris and other forms of rust which corrode the surface, but in uncirculated coins it may be little more than a mellowing of the original lustre. Coins preserved in blue velvet presentation cases often acquire a subtle toning from the dyes in the material.

Pattern   Piece resembling a coin or medal, prepared by the mint to the specifications or on the authorisation of the coin-issuing authority, but also applied to pieces produced by mints when tendering for coinage or medal contracts. Patterns may differ from the final coins as issued in the type of alloy used, but more often they differ in details of the design.

Some of the most famous coins exist only as patterns that were never put into general production.

Pavillon d'or   French gold coin introduced in 1339 and worth 30 **sols**. It derived its name from the elaborate baldaquin or pavilion under which the king Philippe VI was portrayed sitting.

Pellet   Raised circular ornament used as a spacing device between words and abbreviations in the legend of coins and medals. Groups of pellets were also used as ornaments in the interstices of the cross on the reverse of English silver pennies.

Pengö   Unit of currency in Hungary from 1925 till 1946, divided into 100 **filler**.

Penni (plural **pennia**)   Unit of currency in Finland (100 = 1 **markka**).

Penning (plural **penningar**)   Scandinavian equivalent of the **penny** or **pfennig**, minted in Denmark and Sweden from the 14th till the 16th centuries. Various multiples of the penning included the **blaffert** (2p), **dreiling** (3p), **hvid** (4p), **søsling** (6p) **örtug** (8p) and **gros** (9p).

Penny (plural **pennies** or **pence**)   English word for the medieval **denier** or **denarius**, thought to be derived from Penda, King of Mercia, in whose reign silver pendings first appeared. The word passed to Germany as pfanding or pfenning and hence **pfennig**, while in England it became penning or penny. In the written form it was denoted by the letter d (from denarius) until 1971, but since decimalisation it has been denoted by p. The silver penny with the effigy of the ruler on the obverse and a cross on the reverse dates from Offa in the late 8th century. The original **Short Cross** type was followed in the 13th century by the **Long Cross** type which survived till Tudor times. 240 silver pennies were coined from a Saxon or Tower pound of silver, hence the term pennyweight (dwt.) for the smallest unit of weight. Pennies declined in weight, from the original 22½ grains to 7¾ in 1601. The last silver pence for general circulation appeared in 1662 and since then they have only been struck as **Maundy money**. For more than a century thereafter no regal pennies were struck, and the gap was filled by **tokens**, until the first regal copper **cartwheels** were produced in 1797. Bronze was substituted in 1860 and the weight was reduced at the same time. The last pennies in the £sd system appeared in 1967. The much smaller decimal new penny (1971) was worth 2.4 old pence. The word penny is also used colloquially in America to denote the **cent**. Pennies also formed the basis of the coinage systems in many countries of the British Commonwealth.

Pentekontalitron   Sicilian silver coin worth 50 **litrae** or 10 **drachmae**, dating from the late 5th century B.C.

Pentekontedrachm   Gold coin worth 50 **drachmae**, introduced in the reign of Alexander the Great in the 4th century B.C. and minted occasionally by the Hellenistic kingdoms down to the later Ptolemies of Egypt.

Pentenummion   Small Byzantine copper coin worth 5 **nummi** or an eighth of a **follis**, introduced by Anastasius I in A.D. 498 and last minted under Constantine IV in the late 7th century.

Perper (plural **perpera**)   Unit of currency in Montenegro from 1906 till 1918 (= 100 **paras**). Silver 1, 2 and 5 perper coins were minted in 1909–14 and gold 10, 20 and 100 perper coins in 1910.

Pesa   German variant of **paisa**, denoting a copper coin issued in 1890–2 by German East Africa (Tanganyika).

Peseta   Unit of currency in Spain since 1868 (= 100 **centimos**), a diminutive form of **peso**.

Pesewa   Unit of currency in Ghana since 1965, 100 pesewas being worth 1 **cedi**.

Peso   Shortened form of *peso de a ocho reales* (piece of eight **reales**) denoting the large silver coin which is the nearest thing the world has ever come to a universal currency. The first pieces of eight were minted under Ferdinand and Isabella in 1497 and received a tremendous boost from the vast amounts of silver exported from the New World to Europe in the 16th–18th centuries. In 1536 pesos were first struck in Mexico City, the first mint established in the New World. To this day the peso is the principal unit of currency in many Latin American countries: Argentina, Chile, Colombia, Costa Rica, Cuba, the Dominican Republic, Guatemala, Honduras, Mexico, Paraguay, Salvador and Uruguay.

Pessa   Copper coin issued in the Sultanate of Zanzibar in the late 19th century.

Petermännchen   **Billon** or white metal coin worth 8 **pfennigs** or 2 **kreuzers** and portraying St. Peter, minted at Trier, 1625–1764.

Peter's Pence   Name given to a medieval ecclesiastical tax, paid to the Papacy and alluding to St. Peter, first Vicar of Christ, from whom the Popes derive their authority. Payment of this tax was abolished in England in 1366, though some monasteries continued to collect it till 1533. To this day, however, the term denotes freewill offerings to the Church in many Catholic countries. Certain medieval coins of Poland are said to have been minted specifically for this purpose and are known as *Peterspfennige*.

Pfennig   German word, derived from Pfanding, pfenning and ultimately penning (**penny**), signifying originally the silver coins minted in the Carolingian Empire on the model of the Roman **denarius**. The value of the pfennig varied considerably in different parts of the Holy Roman Empire and declined from a silver coin to a copper or bronze piece in the 18th century. In terms of other coins the pfennig was tariffed at 4 to the **kreuzer**, 8 to the **mariengroschen**, 12 to the reichsgroschen, or 286 to the imperial **taler**. It was adopted as the unit in the decimal system of German introduced in 1873 (100 = 1 **mark**).

Philippeioi   Gold **staters** struck from **bullion** obtained from the mines of Mount Pangaeum, the richest source of mineral wealth in ancient Greece. They were minted from 348 B.C. onwards under Philip II of Macedon after whom they were named. These handsome coins portraying Apollo and a two-horse chariot were very popular all over the ancient world and were copied by the barbarian Celtic and Teutonic tribes of northwestern Europe.

Piastre (piastra)   Italian and Levantine word derived from the Spanish **peso** and originally signifying any large silver coin. Silver piastres of this type were minted for circulation in the Ottoman Empire and some of its successor states, such as Egypt, the Lebanon, Morocco, Syria, and Tunisia. It was also the name given to a small bronze coin issued in Cyprus, worth a ninth of an English **shilling** (1879–1955). Trade coins known as commercial piastres were issued by Bologna, Florence, Genoa and the Papal States, and this was followed by France which struck silver piastres for circulation in IndoChina. Silver piastres were minted under Norodom I of Cambodia and to this day the word is synonymous with the Vietnamese **dong**.

Piatyaltynny   Silver coin signifying 5 altyn or 15 **kopeks**, minted under Peter the Great.

Pice   Small coin of India, worth a quarter of an anna or 1/64 of a **rupee**. Pice were struck in copper or bronze for circulation in Bhutan and East Africa as well as many of the Indian princely states.

Pie (pai)   The smallest copper coin of India, worth a third of a **pice** or a twelfth or an **anna**. Copper coins of this denomination were minted in British India from 1862 till 1942 and by Dewas (1888) and Dhar (1887). Coins worth 2 pie (pai) were used in Hyderabad in 1943–8.

Pieces of Eight see Peso.

Piedfort (piefort)   Piece struck with coinage dies on a **flan** of much more than the normal thickness. This practice originated in France in the late 16th century and continues to the present day. In recent years it has been adopted by mints in other countries as a medium for collectors' pieces.

Pile   Lower **die** incorporating the obverse motif, used in striking coins and medals.

Pillar Dollar   Nickname of the Spanish pieces of eight featuring the heraldic columns that symbolised the Pillars of Hercules.

Pingin   Irish for **penny**, inscribed on coins of 1928–68.

Piso   Philippino unit of currency, derived from the **peso**.

Pistole   Originally a nickname for the gold double **escudo** introduced by Charles V of Spain in 1537, it came to be applied to other European gold coins of similar size, notably the **louis d'or** of France (1641) and the 5 **taler** coins of the German states in the 18th–19th centuries. The term was used to denote the gold coins struck under the authority of Lord Ormonde in Ireland during the Civil War (1643–4) and the last issue of gold coins made at the Edinburgh mint (1701). Pistoles and half-pistoles, worth £12 and £6 Scots respectively, were minted from gold dust imported by the ill-fated Darien Company trading with Africa.

Plack   Billon coin struck in Scotland between 1470 and 1590, the name being derived from the French word *plaque*.

Planchet   Alternative term for the **flan** or **blank** used in coin and medal production.

Plappart   see **Blaffert**

Plaque   Term sometimes used for medals struck on a rectangular **flan**.

Plaquette   Diminutive form of **plaque**, signifying a small rectangular medal. It also denotes a billon coin worth 14 **liards** struck by authority of the bishops of Liège from 1755 to 1793.

Plaster   Cast taken from the original model for a coin or medal sculpted by an artist, and used in modern reducing machines in the manufacture of the master **die**.

Plate Money   Large copper plates bearing royal cyphers and values from a half to 10 **dalers** were produced in Sweden between 1643 and 1768. They represented laudable attempts by a country rich in copper to produce a coinage in terms of its silver value, but the net result was far too cumbersome to be practical. The weight of the **daler** plate, for example, ranged from 766 grammes to 1.1 kg, and special carts had to be devised to transport them!

Plated coins   Coins struck in base metal but given a wash of silver or some other precious metal. This expedient was adopted in inflationary times, from the Roman Republic (91 B.C.) till the Tudor period. American cents of 1943 were struck in zinc-coated steel.

Platinum   The noblest of all the precious metals, chemical symbol *Pn*, platinum has a higher specific gravity than gold and a harder, brighter surface than silver. Until an industrial application was discovered in the mid-19th century it was regarded as of little value, and was popular with counterfeiters as a cheap substitute for gold in their forgeries which, with a light gold wash, could be passed off as genuine. It was first used for circulating coins in Russia, the chief source of this metal since 1819, and 3, 6 and 12 **rouble** coins were minted at various times between 1828 and 1845. In recent years platinum has been used for proof versions of coins of the Isle of Man.

Plugged coins   Coins struck predominantly in one metal, but containing a small plug of another. This curious practice may be found in the **farthings** of Charles II (1684–5) and the **halfpence** or farthings of James II (1685–7), which were struck in tin, with a copper plug, to defeat forgers.

Poltina   Russian word used in **money of account** to denote half a **rouble** or 50 **kopeks**, derived from the ingots of that value used as currency from the 13th century onwards. From 1654 the half rouble coin was known as a poltinnik, and this expression appears on the reverse of the 50 kopek coins of 1924–7, but the term poltina appears on the reverse of the half rouble coins of the late 17th and 18th centuries.

Poltura   Hungarian silver coin of the 17th and 18th centuries, also minted in Silesia under Prussian administration.

Poludenga   Russian term signifying half **denga**, struck as a silver coin in the 14th–16th centuries and as a copper coin thereafter. It was popularly known as a poluschka. Other coins with the prefix *polu* (half) were the poluimperial or 5 **rouble** gold coin (1895–7), the polupoltina or quarter rouble, and the polupoluschka or one-eighth **kopek** copper coin in the reign of Peter the Great.

Pond   Dutch word for **pound**, inscribed on the gold coins of that denomination minted by authority of the Transvaal (South African Republic). The first issue (1874) is popularly known as the Burgerspond, from the effigy of President Burgers on the obverse. Gold ponds and half ponds portraying President Kruger were struck from 1892 till 1902. **Emergency money** issued by the Boer guerrillas in 1902 was inscribed **Veld Pond** (Field Pound).

Porcelain money   Tokens made of porcelain were produced by the Meissen pottery in 1920–22 during the postwar inflation in Germany as a form of small **Notgeld**. Both reddish-brown Böttger stoneware and white *bisque* porcelain were used for this purpose and circulated in various towns in Saxony. Porcelain **tokens** also circulated in Thailand from the late 18th century till 1868.

Postage currency   Small paper notes in denominations of 5, 10, 25 and 50 cents, issued by the Federal government in 1862–3 were thus inscribed and had reproductions of postage stamps engraved on them – five 5-cent stamps on the 25¢ notes and five 10¢ stamps on the 50¢ notes. The earliest issue even had perforations in the manner of stamps, though this unnecessary device was soon done away with.

Postage stamps as money   Postage stamps have circulated as money during shortages of coins from the American Civil War (1861–5) onwards. **Encased postage stamps** were used in the United States from 1861 till 1862 when they were superseded by the **Postage Currency** notes, but the same expedient was adopted in Germany, France, Austria, Denmark, Norway, Argentina, Belgium, Greece, Italy and Monaco during or immediately after the First World War. Stamps affixed to special cards have circulated as money in Rhodesia (now Zimbabwe) in 1900, Madagascar and Turkey during the First World War, in Spain during the Civil War and the Philippines during the Japanese occupation. Stamps printed on thick card, with an inscription on the reverse signifying their parity with silver coins, were issued in Russia (1917–18) and also in Armenia, the Crimea and the Ukraine (1918–20). During the Second World War Bundi and Ceylon issued small money cards with contemporary stamps printed on them.

Postal notes or orders   Low-value notes intended for transmission by post and encashable at post offices. They were an extension of the earlier **money order** system, introduced in Britain in 1883, and are now issued by virtually every country.

Potin (French for pewter)   An alloy of copper, tin, lead and silver used as a coinage metal by the Celtic tribes of eastern Gaul at the beginning of the Christian era.

Pound   From the Latin word **pondus**, meaning simply a weight, it became synonymous in medieval English (*phund*) with the Roman **libra**. As a weight, the pound varied from 320 to 560 grammes depending on the material being weighed, and this disparity survived in the troy and avoirdupois systems. As **money of account** the pound was denoted by its Roman initial £ and divided nominally into 20 **solidi** or **shillings** or 240 **denarii** or **pence**, hence the £sd notation used in Britain until 1871. The pound as a unit of weight and money of account traced its descent from the Roman libra, via the Carolingian pound of the Middle Ages to the Saxon pound of the same period. The first gold coin in England of this value was the **sovereign** of 20 **shillings** introduced by Henry VII in 1489. Double and treble sovereigns are known in the form of **piedforts** from the sovereign dies but were probably unique presentation pieces. In ensuing reigns the sovereign varied between 22s 6d and 30s and the need for a denomination worth 20s led to the introduction of the gold pound of 172 grains in 1583. Gold 20-shilling coins in the reign of James I went under such names as sovereign (1603–4), **unite** (1604–12) and **laurel** (1619–25), reflecting the severe fluctuations in the value of gold. Under Charles I the pound was again synonymous with the unite, but during the Civil War silver pounds were minted at Shrewsbury and Oxford. The milled gold coins introduced in 1663 were known as **guineas** but were worth half a pound, £1, £2 and £5. In the 18th century the guinea diverged in value from the traditional pound as the price of gold rose, and the old 20 shilling standard was not restored till the currency reform of 1816 which introduced the sovereign of the present size, weight and fineness. Since the late 17th century paper money in pound denominations and multiples has also been issued. The gold sovereign went out of general circulation in 1914 but despite agitation for the re-introduction of a pound coin in recent years, this has so far been ignored by the British government. Commemorative silver and gold coins with a face value of a pound or its multiples have been issued by Malta and Jersey since 1972, but the first circulating pound was issued by the Isle of Man in 1978 in a high-security base metal known as **virenium**.

Privy mark   Secret mark incorporated in the design of a coin or medal to identify the minter, or even the particular die used. The term is also used moore loosely to denote any small symbol or initials appearing on a coin other than the **mint mark**, and is sometimes applied to the symbols associated with the trial of the **pyx** found on English coins of the 14th–17th centuries. Examples of the different types of privy mark would thus include the initials of the engraver or designer, such as WW (William Wyon) and KG (Kruger Gray) found on British coins; tiny numerals on British sovereigns, and runic lettering on Manx coins identifying the particular dies used. The Millennium logotype appeared as a privy mark on Manx coins issued in 1979 to celebrate the 1000th anniversary of Tynwald, the island's parliament.

Prize coins   Coins of large size and value struck primarily as prizes in sporting contests. This principle dates from the late 5th century B.C. when Syracuse minted **decadrachms** as prizes in the Demareteian Games. The most notable example in modern times is the lengthy series of **talers** and **5-franc** coins issued by the Swiss cantons since 1842 as prizes in the annual shooting festivals, the last of which honoured the Lucerne contest in 1939.

Promissory note   Notes covering loans of money which were then used as a form of paper money by goldsmiths and financiers in medieval Europe. By an Exchequer Order of 1665 they were even made legal tender in England and thus antedate banknotes (of the Bank of England) by some thirty years. The earliest notes were entirely handwritten, but by the 18th century they were printed by copperplate engraving and many 19th century notes were very colourful, incorporating pictorial elements. They declined in importance and were superseded by **banknotes, bills of exchange** and **sight notes**.

Proof   Originally a trial strike testing the **dies**, but now denoting a special collector's version struck with dies that have been specially polished on **flans** with a mirror finish. Presses operating at a very slow speed, or even multi-striking processes, are also used.

Propaganda notes   Paper money containing a political slogan or a didactic element. During the Second World War forgeries of German and Japanese notes were produced by the Allies and additionally inscribed or overprinted with slogans such as "Co-Prosperity Sphere – What is it worth?" (a reference to the Japanese occupied areas of Southeast Asia). Forged dollars with anti-American propaganda were air-dropped over Sicily by the Germans in 1943 and counterfeit pounds with Arabic propaganda over Egypt in 1942–3. Various anti-communist organisations have liberated propaganda forgeries of paper money by balloon over Eastern Europe in recent years.

Provenance mark   Form of **privy mark** denoting the source of the metal used in coins. Examples include the plumes or roses on English coins denoting silver from Welsh or West of England mines, and the elephant or elephant and castle on gold coins denoting **bullion** important by the African Company. Coins inscribed VIGO (1702–3) or LIMA (1745–6) denote bullion seized from the Spaniards by Anglo-Dutch privateers and Admiral Anson respectively. Other provenance marks on English coins include the letters E.I.C. and S.S.C. denoting bullion imported by the East India Company and the South Sea Company.

Pruta (plural **prutot**)   Unit of currency in Israel from 1949 till 1960 (1,000 = 1 Israeli £).

Pseudo coins   Derisory term coined in recent years to signify pieces of precious metal, often struck in proof versions only, aimed at the international investment market. Many of these pieces, though bearing a nominal face value, are not legal tender in the countries purporting to issue them and in many cases they go straight from the overseas mint where they are produced to coin dealers in American and western Europe, without ever appearing in the so-called country of origin.

Pu   Chinese word for a spade, and thus the name given to bronze pieces used as money between 1122 and 255 B.C., from their round-shouldered, square-footed appearance.

Puffin   Small bronze pieces inscribed as puffins or half-puffins and depicting the sea bird of that name were struck in 1929 on behalf of Martin C. Harman whose profile appeared on the obverse. Mr. Harman was prosecuted in England the following year and the coins, intended for circulation on Lundy in the Bristol Channel, were suppressed. A similar issue in bronze and nickel-brass, however, was permitted in 1965.

Pul (puli, puls)   Originally a copper coin of the Golden Horde in the 13th–15th centuries, it was later issued by Russia for use in Turkestan, and is now the unit of currency in Afghanistan (100 = 1 **afghani**).

Punch (puncheon)   Intermediate die whereby working dies can be duplicated from the master die, prior to the striking of coins and medals.

Pya   Unit of currency in Burma since 1952 (100 = 1 **kyat**).

Pyx   Box in which a specimen from every 15 pounds Troy weight of gold and every 60 pounds of silver minted in England is kept for annual trial by weight and assay. Many of the **mint marks** on English coins of the 14th–17th century were in use from one trials till the next and can therefore be used to date them.

Q

Qind (qint, qindarka)   Unit of currency in Albania, signifying 'hundredth' (100 = 1 **lek**).

Qirsh   Alternative spelling of the Arab **girsh** or **guerche** (**grosh**) 20 = 1 Saudi **riyal**).

Quadrans   Large bronze coin of the Roman republic, worth a quarter of an **as**. In the Imperial period it served as the smallest coin in circulation.

Quart   Subsidiary copper coin used by Gibraltar in the 19th century, a variant of the Spanish **cuarto**.

Quart d'écu   French for a quarter écu, the name given to the silver coin worth 15 **sols** struck in 1548 under Henri IV.

Quartenses   Latin word signifying a fourth part or quarter, used to denote a small coin of Silesia worth a quarter **schoter** or 1/24 Prussian **mark**, minted by the Dukes and Bishops of Breslau from 1292 till 1322.

Quarter   American terms for the quarter **dollar** or 25-**cent** coin.

Quartillo   Diminutive of **quarto**, and given to a small Spanish coin of the 18th–19th centuries.

Quartinho   Portuguese term for the quarter **moidore** of the 17th–18th centuries.

Quartje   Dutch diminutive term signifying the quarter **gulden** or 25-**cent** coin.

Quarto   Alternative name for the **cuarto**, a small silver coin used in Spain in the 19th century.

Quartuncia   Latin for 'quarter ounce', the name given to the smallest bronze piece used by the Roman Republic, 220–200 B.C.

Quaternio   Name given to the Roman 4-**aureus** gold coin, minted rarely in the reigns of Augustus Domitian and Philip I.

Quattrino   Small silver coin issued by the Papacy and other Italian states in the 14th–16th centuries. 1 quattrino = 4 piccoli; 5 quattrini = 1 **baiocco**.

Quetzal   Long-tailed tropical bird, the national emblem of Guatemala and the chief unit of currency since 1926 (= 100 centavos).

Quinarius   Silver coin worth 5 **asses** or half a **denarius**, minted from 211 B.C., but rarely issued after the 1st century A.D.

Quincunx   Latin term denoting 5 ounces and used for a coin in the **Aes Grave** series. Coins of this denomination were produced by the tribes of eastern Italy before they came under Roman rule.

Quint   Unit of currency, from the Latin word for fifth, suggested by Gouverneur Morris for the United States, 1783. Silver **patterns** were produced by Benjamin Dudley, worth 500 **units** or half a **mark**.

Quinto di Scudo   Italian for "fifth of a **scudo**", denoting the silver coin worth 20 **baiocchi** and sometimes called a **papetto**, minted by the Papacy in the 19th century.

Quittungen   German word for "receipts", signifying the paper money used in the ghetto of Litzmannstadt (Lodz, Poland) and Theresienstadt (Teresin, Bohemia). Jews kept in these camps were forced to exchange their German, Czech and Polish currency for these receipts. The quittungen of Theresienstadt are also known as "Moses crowns" because they portrayed Moses with the Ten Commandments.

R

Rand   Unit of currency in South Africa since 1961, derived from the Rand near Johannesburg, source of the country's mineral wealth. Rands (= 100 **cents**) are struck in silver for general circulation, but the name is also given to a bullion piece of 1 ounce fine gold known as a **Krugerrand** from the portrait of Paul Kruger on the obverse.

Rappen   Unit of currency in Switzerland since the Middle Ages, but now the 100th of a Swiss **franc**. The derivation of the word is uncertain, but probably from the Swiss word *rapp* meaning dark-coloured, applied originally to the so-called black *bracteates* of inferior silver. By the 15th century the name was given to the curious square pfennigs of the Swiss cantons. In the Helvetic Republic of 1799 it was tariffed at a tenth of a **batzen** and thus became the lowest unit in the decimal system.

Real   Silver coin adopted by Spain and Portugal in the mid-14th century. It enjoyed varying fortunes thereafter and reflected the comparative states of the economy in these countries. Whereas it became the mainstay of the Spanish currency, especially in its multiple, the **peso** of 8 reales, it declined in value in Portugal until it signified a small bronze coin, later superseded by the **reis**, which was, in fact the plural form in Portuguese and denoted multiples of the real, from 10 to 10,000. Spanish reales were usually minted in silver (*real de plata*) but billon coins were struck in the reign of Joseph Bonaparte (1808–13) and known as *real de vellon*. The *real d'or* (gold real) was a gold coin issued in the Spanish Netherlands in 1487 and the model for the English **sovereign** of 1489.

Rechenpfennig   German term signifying "accountancy penny" and denoting **jetons** used by accountants from the 13th till the late 17th centuries. These coin-like pieces were manufactured mostly in Nuremberg.

Reducing machine   Device invented about 1819 by M. Collas of Paris and operating on the pantographic principle. By this means the original plaster relief sculpted by an artist on a large scale can be reduced to the required size. In its original form this machine transferred the details to a coin-sized **plaster** which was then metallised and transformed into a master punch from which subsidiary **dies** could be made, but modern machines cut the master die direct, using a special stylus. Equipment of this type was adopted by the Royal Mint in 1824 and by the mid-19th century had revolutionised coin production everywhere. By doing away with the need for the engraver it freed coin design from traditional restraints, but it has also been blamed for the somewhat stereotyped quality of modern coin design.

Reeding   Security edging on coins, consisting of close vertical ridges. As a rule, this appears all round the edge but New Zealand's 50 cent (1967) and the Isle of Man's £1 (1978) have segments of reeding alternating with a plain edge, to help blind and partially sighted persons to identify these coins.

Reichs   Prefix meaning "Imperial", applied to many coins from the Middle Ages onwards from reichstaler to **reichsmark**.
See entries under **mark**, **taler**, etc.

Reichskreditkassen   German for "state credit bank". Collectors' name for the paper notes produced for the use of German troops on active service during the Second World War in occupied territories.

Reichsmark, Reichspfennig   Decimal system adopted by Germany in 1924 (100 Rpf = 1RM) following the currency reform of that year. This system continued through the Nazi period (1933–45) and coins and notes of the Allied occupation (1945–8) were similarly inscribed. The prefix "reichs" was dropped in 1948 when the currency was again reformed and the Bank Deutscher Länder established.

Reis   Portuguese plural form of **real**, the unit of currency used in Portugal till 1910 and in Brazil till 1942.

Relief   Raised part of the **obverse** and **reverse** of coins and medals.

Rentenmark, rentenpfennig   Short-lived currency adopted by Germany in 1923 as a means of ending the hyper-inflation. A new issue of money was made, guaranteed by mortgage bonds funded on real estate. These notes, known as rentenmarks, were secured by interest-bearing bonds and could be automatically converted into them. The transitional currency gave the government the required breathing space, and paved the way for the introduction of the **reichsmark** late in 1924. Bronze 2-rentenpfennig and aluminium-bronze 5-, 10- and 50-rentenpfennig, and rentenmark notes were issued in 1923–4. 10-rentenpfennig coins dated 1925 are rare **mis-strikes**.

Restrike   Coin, medal or token produced from **dies** subsequent to the original issue. Usually restrikes are made long after the original and can often be identified by marks caused by damage, pitting or corrosion of the dies after they were taken out of service.

Retrograde   Term describing inscriptions running from right to left, or with the letters in a mirror image, thought to arise from unskilled die-cutters failing to realise that inscriptions have to be engraved in negative form to achieve a positive strike. Retrograde inscriptions are common on ancient Greek coins, but also found on Roman and Byzantine coins.

Reul   Gaelic for **real**, inscribed on the **sixpence** of Ireland, 1928–69.

Reverse   The side of a coin or medal regarded as of lesser importance; in colloquial parlance, the "tails" side.

Rial   Variant of **riyal**, an Arabic currency unit since the Middle Ages and modelled on the Spanish **real**. In Morocco

the rial worth 500 **mazunas** survived till 1919, whereas Iran
adopted the rial of 100 **dinars** in 1932 and Muscat and Oman
introduced the rial saidi of 1,000 **baizas** in 1970.

Rider   Gold coin introduced by James III of Scotland in
1475, along with its half and quarter and tariffed at 23
shillings sterling. It was discontinued in 1483 but was revived
by James VI for his seventh gold coinage (1593–1601) and
was then worth 100 shillings. Half riders were minted in the
same period. The name is derived from the equestrian portrait
of the king on the obverse.

Riel   Unit of currency in Cambodia and subsequently the
Khmer Republic, since 1955 (= 100 cents). A series of seven
gold coins from 5,000 to 100,000 riels was issued in 1974.

Rigsbankdaler   Danish for "state bank dollar", denoting
a silver coin introduced in 1813, worth half a **speciedaler** and
divided into 96 *rigsbankskilling*.

Rigsdaler   Danish silver coin, introduced in 1854 in place
of the **rigsbankdaler**. On the adoption of the decimal system
of the **Scandinavian Monetary Union** (1873), the rigsdaler
was tariffed at 2 **kroner**.

Rijder   Gold coin of the Netherlands, modelled on the
French *franc à cheval* and first issued by Guelderland in 1581,
followed by Friesland (1583) and the United Provinces
(1606). Large silver coins with a similar motif and known as
rijderdaalder were also issued from 1581 and survived till the
late 18th century.

Rijksdaalder   Dutch for "state dollar", the name given to
a large silver coin modelled on the **taler** of the German Empire
and issued by various provinces from 1581. From 1659 it was
synonymous with the silver *ducat* and has its modern counterpart in the 2½-**gulden** coins of the Netherlands.

Riksdaler   Swedish for 'state dollar', the name given to the
specietaler introduced in 1775 in the monetary reforms mark-
ing a switch from copper to silver. The riksdaler was tariffed
at 3 **dalers** SM (silver money) or 48 **skilling**. Fluctuations in
the value of state paper money in the mid-19th century led to

the issue of the riksdaler of 1844–59 whose reverse was inscribed 1RD. SPEC. / 4 RD. RIKSM, indicating the value of the coin in terms of the debased paper riksdalers. Later coins (1861–71) bore the value in *Riksmunten* (state coin).

Rin   Diminutive coin of Japan, worth a tenth of a **sen**. Bronze 5-rin coins were minted in 1873–88 and 1916–19.

Ring Dollar see **Holey Dollar**

Ringgit   Unit of currency in Malaysia, synonymous with the dollar (= 100 **cents** or **sen**).

Rio   Japanese unit of silver weight, used as **money of account** till 1870.

Rixdaler   Alternative form of **rijksdaalder**.

Riyal (ryal)   Variant of the Arab **rial**, used by Iraq (= 200 **fils**). Silver riyals were issued in 1932.

Rosa Americana   Name given to a series of **tokens** produced by William Wood for circulation in the American colonies, 1722–33, in denominations of halfpenny, penny and twopence. The name is derived from the reverse showing a rose with the Latin legend *Rosa Americana – Utile Dulci* (American rose – the useful with the sweet).

Rose Noble   English gold coin introduced by Edward III in 1464 when the **noble** was raised in value from 6s 8d to 10 shillings. It derived its name from the rose on the reverse. Half and quarter rose nobles were also minted.

Rouble   Russian unit of currency, derived from the verb *rubit'*, to cut, and alluding to its origin as a strip or bar of silver cut into convenient lengths and circulated as a primitive form of money in the Middle Ages. The rouble was adopted as the principal unit by the Empress Helena in the monetary reform of 1534 and divided into 100 **kopeks**, the world's first decimal system.

Royal d'or   French 24 carat gold coin minted between 1326 and 1369, worth 25 **sols**, and portraying Charles IV or Charles V on the obverse.

Royalin (plural **royaliner**)   Small silver coin issued at Tranquebar, India, by the Danish colonial administration from 1755 till 1807. On par with the **fano**, 8 royaliner = 1 **rupee**; 18 royaliner = 1 **speciedaler**.

Rupee   Indian unit of currency derived from the Sanskrit word *rupa*, a herd of cattle, and serving first as barter currency and later as **money of account**. The earliest coins of this denomination were struck by Sher Shah in the 10th century. In its present guise, however, it dates from 1676 when silver rupees were issued by the East India Company. Nickel has been used since 1947, though silver 10 or 20 rupee coins have appeared for commemorative purposes in recent years. Under British administration the rupee was worth 16 **annas**, or a fifteenth of a gold **mohur**. Since 1957 it has been worth 100 **naye paisa** and, since 1964, 100 **paisa**. The rupee system of coinage was also used in Afghanistan, Bhutan, Burma, Ceylon (= 100 **cents**), East Africa (= 200 **cowries**), Mauritius and Seychelles (= 100 cents), Nepal, Tibet and Saudi Arabia.

Rupia   Italian or Portuguese variant of **rupee**, inscribed on the coinage formerly used in Italian East African and the Portuguese settlements in India (Goa, Diu and Damao).

Rupiah   Unit of currency in Indonesia since 1950 (= 100 **sen**). Only paper money was issued in rupiah denominations till 1970 when inflation resulted in a series of coins in aluminium or cupro-nickel, from 1 to 100 rupiah. Silver and gold coins from 200 to 25,000 rupiah appeared the same year.

Rupie   Unit of currency in German East Africa (Tanganyika) from 1888 till 1914. Originally tariffed at 64 **pesa**, it was retariffed at 100 **heller** in 1904.

Ryal   Alternative name for the **rose noble** of 10 **shillings**, introduced in 1464 by Edward IV. Half and quarter ryal gold coins were minted as well, up to 1470 when it was dropped in favour of a resumption of the **angel** (third pound) system. It was briefly revived as a gold coin worth 15 shillings in the last years of Elizabeth I (1583–1600). Gold coins known as the *rose ryal* and the *spur ryal*, respectively worth 30s and 15s (revalued at 33s and 16s 6d in 1612) were minted under James I. Both coins returned to their original value in 1619 and continued till 1625.

Rytterpenninge   (Danish for "rider penny") the name given to various coins of Denmark and the Hanseatic cities of northern Germany in the 17th century, based on the Russian denninge and depicting a horseman on the obverse.

S

Saiga Small, dumpy silver coin of the Merovingians, struck by authority of Charles Martel at Arles and Marseilles and worth a quarter of a **tremissis**.

Salut d'or French gold coin deriving its name from the scene of the Annunciation on the obverse. It was briefly issued by Charles VI in 1421, but served as the model for the English half **noble** and was thereafter struck under the authority of Henry V and Henry VI in the French towns under English control.

Saluto d'oro Gold coin, depicting the Annunciation, first issued by Charles I of Anjou for his Neapolitan domains in the late 13th century. Silver **grossi** of similar appearance were issued by Charles I and Charles II of Anjou.

Sampietrino Copper coin worth 2½ **baiocchi** introduced in the Papal states in 1795 and deriving its name as a diminutive of St. Peter, portrayed on the obverse.

Sandwich Coin **blanks** or strip composed of layers of different metals. This practice was adopted by the United States in 1965 to supersede silver. Half dollars from 1965 to 1970 were struck in a sandwich whose outer layers were an alloy of 80% silver and 20% copper, bonded to an inner core of 21% silver and 79% copper. The dime, quarter (since 1965) and half dollar (since 1971) were struck in a sandwich whose outer layers were an alloy of 75% copper and 25% nickel, bonded to a core of pure copper. The Eisenhower dollars issued since 1971 have been available in both kinds of sandwich, respectively denoted by the D or S **mint marks**. Other coins struck in a sandwich of different alloys include the West German pfennig denominations since 1950 (bronze or brass clad steel).

Sanese d'ora   Gold coin of Siena, minted between 1340 and 1553, modelled on the fiorino of Florence.

Santims (plural **santimi, santimu**)   Unit of currency in Latvia, 1922–40 (100 = 1 **lats**). The name was derived from the phonetic spelling of the French **centime**.

Sapèque (Sepek)   Annamese unit of currency based on the Chinese **cash**. The name comes from the Malay *sa paku* (one chain-link) and alludes to the custom of stringing these holed coins together.

Sarrazzino   Crusader gold coin of the mid-13th century, struck in imitation of Arab **dinars** completed with Kufic inscriptions from the Koran, but incorporating a tiny Christian cross. The name is derived from the Italian word for Saracen.

Satang   Decimal unit in the Thai monetary system. Cupro-nickel coins from 2½ to 20 satangs were introduced in 1897 (100 = 1 **tical**). Since 1950, 100 satangs = 1 **baht**, and coins have been minted in tin, bronze or aluminium bronze.

Satirical medal   Medal cast or struck for political purposes, ridiculing the opposition by means of parody, caricature or symbolic motifs. Numerous examples were produced in various parts of Europe from the early 17th century onwards, often incorporating anti-Catholic or anti-semitic elements. Among the more noteworthy British examples were those lampooning the Earl of Bute over the treatment of John Wilkes (1764–74), the **Cumberland Jack** satirising the unpopular Duke of Cumberland (1837) and the Peterloo Massacre medal (1819). This art form attained its zenith in Germany during the First World War, in the hands of accomplished medallic satirists like Karl Götz, A. Löwenthal and Ludwig Gies, but the medal was soon superseded by more ephemeral media such as postcards and cartoons. There was a brief resurgence of satirical medals in America in the wake of the Watergate scandal (1972–3).

Scandinavian Monetary Union   Convention between Denmark and Sweden (1873), subsequently joined by

Norway (1875), which resulted in a common currency based on the **krone** of 100 öre. Parity broke down during the First World War and the Union was dissolved in 1924, but the krone-öre decimal system survives in Scandinavian countries to this day.

Sceat   Anglo-Saxon word meaning treasure (cf. German *Schatz*), used as **money of account** in Kent early in the 7th century as the twentieth part of a **shilling** or Merovingian gold **tremessis**. As a silver coin, it dates from about A.D. 680–700 and weighed about 20 grains, putting it on par with the Merovingian **denier** or silver **penny**. Sceats spread to other parts of England in the 8th century but tended to decline in weight and value, but from *c*. 760 it was gradually superseded by the silver penny minted under Offa and his successors.

Scellino   Unit of currency in Somalia since 1962, derived from the Italian word for **shilling**.

Schilling   German variant of **shilling**, used as the unit of currency in many parts of Switzerland, Austria and southern Germany from the late Middle Ages. It survives to this day in the schilling of 100 **groschen** used by Austria since 1925.

Schoter or Skot   Small coin of the duchy of Silesia and the bishopric of Breslau worth four **quartenses** or a sixth of a Prussian **mark**, minted in the late medieval period.

Schwaren   Unit of currency in the Hanseatic city of Bremen from the late 15th century, 24 schwaren being worth a **mark** weighing 3¼ lot. Coins in schwaren denominations were also struck in the grand-duchy of Oldenburg.

Scrip   Collector's term for paper money of restricted validity of circulation, e.g. military scrip used in canteens and post exchanges.

Scudo (plural scudi)   Italian word, from Latin *scutum*, meaning a shield, and hence the armorial device featured on many medieval coins. More specifically, however, it came to be applied to silver coins of **taler** or **crown** size, or gold coins modelled on the French écu. Scudi were minted in many parts of Italy till the 19th century, and also served as the unit of currency in Malta under the Knights of St. John, and in several Latin American countries in the early 19th century (Bolivia, Chile, Costa Rica, Ecuador and Peru).

Scyphate   Term derived from the Greek word *skypha* (skiff or small boat) and denoting coins of the Byzantine Empire with a concave **flan**.

Seignorage (seigneurage)   Royalty or percentage paid by persons bringing **bullion** to a mint for conversion into coin, but nowadays synonymous with the royalty paid by mints in respect of the precious metal versions of coins sold direct to collectors. It arises from the medieval right of the king to a small portion of the proceeds of a mint, and amounted to a tax on moneying. It has also been applied to the money accruing to the state when the coinage is re-issued in an alloy of lesser fineness, as, for example, the debased sovereigns of Henry VIII in 20 carat instead of 23 carat gold, the king's treasury collecting the difference.

Semis (from Latin *semi as* = half as); plural **semisses**   A large bronze or aurichalcum piece worth half an **As Libra** or Roman pound, or six unciae, in the early Roman imperial period.

Semuncia   Roman **Aes Grave** coin worth 1/24 of an **as**, minted between 270 and 180 B.C.

Sen   Oriental variant of **cent**, first used in the Japanese decimal system from 1868 onward (100 sen = 1 **yen**) but extended since the 1940s to Brunei, Cambodia, Indonesia and Malaysia.

Sene   Polynesian variant of **cent**, used in Western Samoa (100 sene = 1 **tala**).

Sengi   Unit of currency in Zaïre since 1971; 100 sengi = 1 (li) **kuta**; 100 (ma) kuta = 1 **zaïre**.

Seniti   Variant of **cent**, used in Tonga since 1967 (100 seniti = 1 **pa'anga**).

Sent (plural **senti**)   Unit of currency adopted by Estonia in 1928 (100 senti = 1 **kroon**).

Senti   Unit of currency in Tanzania since 1966 (100 senti = 1 Tanzanian shilling or **shilingi**).

Sentimo   Philippino variant of the Spanish **centimo**, adopted in 1967 (100 sentimos = 1 **piso**).

Sequin   Anglicised version of the gold **zecchino** of Venice.

Serebrnik (plur serebrniki)   Medieval southern Slavic word for silver, denoting Bulgarian coins closely modelled on Byzantine contemporaries of the 10th–11th centuries.

Series   Term applied to sets of medals of a thematic character, which first became fashionable in the early 18th century. Jean Dassier pioneered the medallic series in the 1720s with his set of 72 medals portraying the rulers of France till Louis XV. The idea was developed by J. Kirk, Sir Edward Thomason, J. Mudie and A. J. Stothard in Britain, and by Moritz Fuerst and Amedée Durand in Europe. The fashion died out in the 19th century, but has been revived in America and Europe since 1964.

Serrated coin   Coin having a notched or toothed edge, rather like a cogwheel. Coins of this type, struck in **electrum**, are known from Carthage in the 2nd century B.C., and some silver **denarii** of Rome in the 2nd century A.D. also come into this category.

Sertum   Bhutanese gold coin issued since 1966 on par with the British **sovereign**.

Sesena   Small silver coin minted in Spain in the late medieval period. The name is derived from the word for six and denoted a value of 6 **denari** or half a **sol**.

Sesino   Italian counterpart of the **sesena**, struck in billon or copper in many parts of Italy from the 14th till the 18th centuries.

Sestertius   (Sometimes anglicised as **sesterce**) **Money of account** in Roman times, derived from *semis tertius* (third half) and indicating 2½ **asses** or a quarter of a **denarius**. In Imperial times the gold **aureus** was worth 100 sestertii.

Sestino   Italian diminutive from "sixth", denoting a small billon coin of Naples worth a sixth of a **tornese**, minted in the reign of Ferdinand III of Aragon. Copper sestini were also struck during the French campaign against Naples in 1502–3.

Severin (severinus)   **Money of account** used in financial transactions in Germany during the 18th century, and derived from the French **souverain d'or**.

Sexagesimal system   Monetary system in which the principal unit is divided into 60 parts. The oldest system in the Western world was based on the gold **talent** of 60 **minae** and the mina of 60 **shekels**. In medieval Europe 60 **groschen** were worth a fine **mark**; in England from 1551, the silver coinage was based on the **crown** of 60 **pence**, and in the south German states till 1873 the **gulden** was worth 60 **kreuzers**.

Shahi (chahi)   Unit of currency in Persia, derived from the emperor (*shahinshah*), used till 1932. 50 **dinars** = 1 shahi; 20 shahis = 1 **kran**.

Shekel   Originally an ancient western Asiatic unit of weight, worth the sixtieth part of a **mina**, it was used as money of account in biblical times. Silver shekels were first minted during the First Jewish Revolt (A.D. 66–70), with quarter shekels in bronze, and re-appeared during the Second Revolt (132–135). These shekels provided the motifs for the Israeli 250 and 500 **prutot** of 1949 and the 5 **agorot** of 1960. Pidyon shekels – silver coins intended for the redemption of the first-born – have also been struck by Israel since 1970, and often shekels of the 1st and 2nd centuries have been reproduced.

Shilingi   Tanzanian unit of currency since 1966 (= 100 senti).

Shilling   Originally money of account in Carolingian times to denote 12 **pennies** or the twentieth part of a pound of gold, it was first struck as a coin in 1504 in the reign of Henry VII, the first English coin to diverge from medieval tradition in its design. It continued as a silver coin of 12 pence till 1946 and thereafter in cupro-nickel till 1967. Though superseded in 1968 by the 5 new pence coin, the shillings minted since

1816 are still legal tender in Britain. From 1937 to 1967 shillings were struck in Scottish and English versions, differing in their reverse motifs, but both circulated freely throughout the United Kingdom. The shilling and its multiples also formed an important part of the coinage in many countries in the British Commonwealth. Decimal shillings of 100 cents were the unit of currency in East Africa (Kenya, Tanganyika, Tanzania and Uganda) but everywhere else it formed a part of the £sd system.

Shin Plasters   Derisory term applied originally to the Continental currency notes issued during the American War of Independence, the fractional currency notes of the Civil War period and also the low-denomination notes of Canada between 1870 and 1935.

Shokang   Small copper coin of Tibet minted till 1953. 1½ shokang = 1 **trangka** or **tangka**; 10 shokang = 1 **srang**.

Short Cross Penny   Term denoting the silver penny of England introduced by Henry II in 1180 and minted till 1247 when it was replaced by the Long Cross type. The termination of the arms of the cross on the reverse well within the circumference encouraged the dishonest practice of **clipping** the silver.

Siege money   see **Obsidional money**

Sight note   Bill of exchange payable "at sight" on presentation, or so many days or months after sight, the period being calculated from the date of sighting. They can be recognised by a formula such as "At . . . sight pay this first of exchange . . ." or "Thirty days after sight of this our second of exchange . . ." Sight notes are usually larger and more elaborate than **cheques**.

Siglos (plural **sigloi**)   Greek variant of the semitic **money of account** (**shekel**), minted as a silver coin by the Achaemenids in Persia as the twentieth part of the gold **daric**. Half and double sigloi were also struck.

Silbergroschen   Unit of currency in Prussia and other north German states, tariffed at 12 **pfennigs** or a thirtieth of a **taler**.

Silbergulden   Silver coin of southern Germany worth two-thirds of a **taler** or 60 **kreuzers**, many different types being minted in the 19th century.

Siliqua   Silver coin worth a twentieth of a **solidus**, introduced by Constantine the Great in 323 but gradually debased in weight and fineness till the late 7th century. Siliquae were struck at Rome, Ravenna, Carthage and Syracuse as well as Constantinople during the Byzantine Empire.

Silver   Precious metal, chemical symbol *Ag* from Latin *Argentum*, used as a coinage metal from the 6th century B.C. to the present day. **Sterling** silver denotes an alloy of .925 fine silver with .075 copper. Fine silver alloys used over the past 2,500 years have ranged from .880 to .960 fine, but base silver has also been all too common. British coins from 1920 to 1946 were struck in .500 fine silver, while alloys of lesser fineness are known as **billon** or vellon. Silver alloyed with gold produces **electrum**, used for the earliest coinage of the western world, the **staters** of Lydia in the 7th century B.C. Since 1970 silver as a medium for circulating coinage has virtually disappeared, yet the volume of silver coins for sale to collectors has risen considerably in recent years.

Sixpence   English silver coin introduced in 1551 and worth half a **shilling**. Sixpences were minted in silver till 1946 and in cupro-nickel till 1967. After decimalisation in 1971 the coin was retained in circulation with a nominal value of 2½ new pence, but was demonetised in 1980. Sixpences were also minted in Australia (1910–63), South Africa (1923–60), New Zealand (1933–65) and other British Commonwealth countries in the **sterling** area.

Sizain   French billon coin worth half a **douzain**, issued from 1500 to 1547. Copper sizains were also issued for use in Perpignan under the Emperor Charles V in the mid-16th century and as **obsidional currency** during the siege of Barcelona by the French in 1642.

Skilling   Scandinavian variant of **shilling**, used as money of account from the Middle Ages as 1/48 of a **daler**, but appearing as an actual coin in Denmark (from 1442), Norway (from the late 15th century) and Sweden (only from 1802). Sweden replaced it by the decimal **ore** (worth half a skilling) in 1858 and this paved the way for Denmark and Norway to follow suit in 1873–5.

Skit note   Piece of paper masquerading as a banknote. It differs from a **counterfeit** in that its design parodies that of a genuine note, often for political or satirical reasons. Others were produced as April Fools' Day jokes or a form of Valentine (e.g. the Bank of Lovers). In recent years they have been produced as advertising gimmicks, or as coupons permitting a discount off the list price of goods.

Sol   French money of account, derived from the Roman **solidus** and used in the £sd system of the Middle Ages as the twentieth part of a Carolingian pound. The first silver coin of this value was the **gross tournois** (1266), and later coins of this value were the gros de trois blancs and the **douzain**. In the 17th century it depreciated in value, and was minted in billon and copper or brass by the time of the Revolution. As the **sou**, it degenerated to the bronze 5-**centime** coin or twentieth of a **franc** minted from 1853 to 1921. The sol (plural soles) was adopted as the unit of currency by Peru in 1863, deriving its name from the sun which is the Peruvian national emblem. 100 **centavos** = 1 sol; 10 soles = 1 **libra**.

Soldo (plural **soldi**)   Italian money of account, derived from the Roman **solidus**, and used in the Middle Ages to denote 12 **denari**. Silver soldi were first minted in Bologna in the late 12th century and thereafter spread to Genoa, Venice, Milan and other cities of northern Italy. It survived in Lombardy and Venetia under Austrian rule as late as 1866 (100 soldi = 1 **florin**).

Solidus   Latin adjective meaning solid, first applied to a Roman gold coin minted in A.D. 309 under Constantine the Great, smaller than the **aureus** and tariffed at 72 to the **pound**. In western Europe it was superseded by the gold **tremissis**, but retained as **money of account**, whereas the Byzantine Empire used it as the principal unit of currency, striking silver solidi till the 15th century.

Solot   Minor copper coin of Siam (Thailand) worth half an **att**; 128 solots = **1 baht** or **tical.**

Somalo   Unit of currency in Somalia from 1950 till 1962 (= 100 **centesimi**).

Sösling   Danish diminutive form of six, denoting a small silver coin worth 6 **pfennigs**, first minted in 1424 under Eric of Pomerania, but last appearing as a copper coin in 1651. Half-**skilling** coins known by this name were also issued in Norway under John II (1481–1513).

Sou   Corruption of **sol**, used mainly in France to denote the copper or bronze 5-**centime** piece introduced during the French Revolution. Many of the copper tokens issued in French-speaking Canada, such as the famous **bouquet sou**, were thus inscribed.

Souverain d'or   French variant of the English **sovereign**, denoting a gold coin issued in the Netherlands from 1612 till the late 18th century, and worth 6 **gulden.**

Sovereign   Word derived from the Latin **supremus**, signifying the English monarch. The name was first given to a gold coin of 20 **shillings** in 1489 under Henry VII. In its present form, as the most widely used bullion coin, it dates from 1816. A curious feature of the sovereign is the absence of any notation of value, a characteristic of all British gold coins. Sovereigns and half-sovereigns were also minted in colonial branch mints and can be recognised by the **mint-marks** M (Melbourne), P (Perth), S (Sydney), C (Canada = Ottawa), I (India = Calcutta) and SA (South Africa = Pretoria). This practice ceased in 1932.

Spade Guinea   Nickname of the British **guinea** of 1787–99, from the spade-shaped shield on the reverse.

Special Cheque   Cheque printed for the use of large firms and other organisations, in which the name, trademark and even advertising matter of the company occupies the major part and the name of the bank is reduced to a secondary position.

Specie   Financial term denoting money in the form of precious metals (silver and gold), usually struck as coin, as opposed to money in the form of paper notes and bills of exchange. It occurs in the name of some European coins (e.g. **speciedaler, speciestaler, speciesducat**) to denote the use of fine silver or gold.

Specimen   Term adopted by the Royal Mint to signify a striking of base metal coins in a finer quality than the normal circulating version but not up to proof standard. Specimen quality is used in cased sets for sale direct to collectors, and is similar to the diamond or library finish used by the Pobjoy Mint.

Spintriae   Metal tokens produced in Roman Imperial times, with erotic motifs, thought to have been tickets of admission to brothels.

Spit   Copper or iron rod used as a primitive form of currency in the Mediterranean area. The Greek word *belos* meant a spit, dart or bolt, and from this came the word **obolos** used for the coin worth a sixth of a **drachma**.

Srang   Unit of currency in Tibet up to 1953. Silver coins of 1, 1½, 3, 5 and 10 srang and gold 20 srang coins were struck from 1909 onwards. The srang was worth 10 **shokang** or 6⅔ **tangka**.

Stater   Greek unit of weight, used to denote coins of **electrum** or gold minted from the 7th century B.C. onwards all over the Mediterranean area, and even copied by the barbarian tribes of northern Europe and Britain. Silver staters ranged in value from 2 to 4 **drachmae** and were minted in Macedon, Thrace, Sicily and southern Italy.

Steel   Refined and tempered form of iron, used as a coinage metal in the 20th century. Zinc-coated steel **cents** were issued by the United States (1943) but in the form known as acmonital (nickel-steel) it has been extensively used for the coinage of postwar Italy. Other alloys of nickel and steel have been used for coins of the Philippines (1944–5) and Romania since 1963.

Stella   Pattern coin worth four **dollars**, produced by the United States Mint in 1879–80. The reverse showed a five-pointed star inscribed "One Stella". These **patterns** were struck in gold, copper, aluminium and white metal and are extremely rare.

Sterling   Word of uncertain origin denoting money of a standard weight and fineness, and hence the more general meaning of recognised worth. The traditionally accepted derivation from the Easterlings, north German merchants who settled in London in the 13th century and produced silver **pennies** of uniform fineness, is unlikely since the term has been found in documents a century earlier. A more plausible explanation is from Old English *steorling* – "little coin with a star", alluding to Viking pennies with this device, or even as a diminutive form of **stater**. Sterling silver denotes silver of .925 fineness.

Stone money   Primitive currency in the form of large stone discs, used in West Africa in the pre-colonial period, and in the Pacific island of Yap (Caroline Islands) as recently as 1940.

Stotinka (plural **stotinki**)   Bulgarian word for hundredth, denoting the subsidiary coinage in use since 1881. 100 stotinki = 1 **lev**.

Stuber   German variant of the Dutch **stuiver**, denoting the subsidiary coinage used in many parts of northwestern Germany from the late 15th century till the mid-18th century, and variously tariffed at 24 to the **goldgulden**, 6 to the **schilling** or 60 to the **reichstaler**.

Stuiver   Small coin of the Netherlands from medieval times, and used to this day to denote the 5-cent piece. Stuivers were also issued in Dutch colonial possessions, such as Ceylon and Curacao.

Styca   Name given to the debased silver **sceats** of Northumbria in the 8th century A.D.

Styver   Small silver coin of Sweden, worth an öre, minted in the mid-17th century. The term was later used for the 5 or 6 öre coins of the early 18th century and the coin of 1776 tariffed at a quarter *skilling riksgäld* (state money) or a sixth *skilling banco*.

Sucre   Unit of currency in Ecuador since 1884, named after Antonio José de Sucre (1795–1830).

Sueldo   Spanish variant of **soldo**, equated with the **real**. Silver coins from a quarter to 8 sueldos were produced in Bolivia, prior to the currency reform of 1864, and in the Argentinian province of Rio de la Plata from 1815 to 1832.

Sycee   Silver pieces cast in the form of shoes, used as barter currency in China and the East Indies in various sizes and weights from a tenth of a **tael** to 100 taels.

Syli   Unit of currency in Guinea (= 100 **cauri**). Aluminium 1, 2 and 5 syli coins have been issued since 1971.

T

Tackoe   Silver coinage of the Gold Coast, introduced by the British African Company in 1796. 8 tackoe = 1 **ackey**, and coins of 1, 2 and 4 tackoe were issued.

Tael   Chinese unit of weight corresponding to the European ounce and sometimes referred to as a **liang**. It was a measure of silver varying between 32 and 39 grammes. In the 19th century it served as **money of account**, 100 British or Mexican trade dollars being worth 72 tael. The term has also been loosely applied to the Chinese silver **yüan**, although this was worth only .72 tael, or 7 **mace** and 2 **candareens**. 10 **candareens** = 1 **mace**; 10 mace = 1 tael.

Taka   Unit of currency adopted by Bangladesh in 1972 (= 100 **paisa**). A cupro-nickel coin of this denomination appeared in 1975 to publicise the national family planning campaign.

Tala   Polynesian word for **dollar**, inscribed on coins of that value issued by Western Samoa since 1967 and the Tokelau Islands since 1980.

Talari   Ethiopian unit of currency, derived from the **Maria Theresa taler**. The Menelik talari of 1894–1903 was worth 16 **guerches** (**grosh**), while the talari introduced in 1931 was worth 100 **matonás**.

Talent (talanton)   Greek gold unit of weight, equivalent of 60 silver **minae**.

Taler (thaler)   Large silver coin minted extensively in the German states from the 16th to the late 19th centuries. The name was shortened from **Joachimstaler**, derived from Joachimstal (Jachymov, Bohemia) where the Counts of

Schlick minted the first coins from silver mined there. The taler rapidly ousted the earlier **guldiner** and **guldengroschen** as the principal unit in the Holy Roman Empire. Its influence spread far beyond the Empire as is evident in the numerous currency units derived from it: **dala, daler, daalder, dollar, tala, talari, tallero**. Though largely superseded in the 19th century by the **gulden** and the **mark** it survived, in the guise of the **Maria Theresa taler**, as a **trade coin** in the Middle East till recent times.

Talirion   Modern Greek word, derived from the **taler**, and denoting the silver 5-**drachmae** coins minted by Greece between 1833 and 1876.

Tallero   Italian variant of **taler**, denoting large silver coins struck from the late 16th century in Mantua and Florence and subsequently adopted by Venice and Ragusa. It was last minted by Italy in 1918 for use in Eritrea (= 100 cents), the design of both obverse (female bust) and reverse (arms) being a blatant copy of the Maria Theresa **taler** with which it was meant to compete.

Tambac-tron   Silver coin minted under the kings of Annam from 1820 till 1883.

Tambala   Unit of currency in Malawi since 1971. 100 tambala = 1 **kwacha**.

Tanga   Small coin, originally in silver but from 1765 in copper, circulating in the Portuguese settlements in India since 1615 as a fifth of a **xeraphim**. In the 19th and 20th centuries it was on par with the **anna** of British India till its abolition in 1958.

Tangka (**trangka**)   Silver coin of Tibet and Nepal, struck from the mid-16th century till 1947. 1½ **shokang** = 1 tangka; 6⅔ tangka = 1 **srang**.

Tankah   Hindu unit of weight and **money of account**. Silver coins of this value were first minted at Delhi in the early 13th century, and as a gold coin in the Deccan in the 14th century.

Tarin   Silver coin introduced under Ferdinand II of Aragon in the late 15th century for use in Naples and Sicily, and worth 2 **carlini**. Tarins were struck at Messina till the late 18th century.

Taro (plural **tari**)   Tiny gold coin weighing about a gramme, issued by the Siculo-Norman, Angevin and Hohen-staufen rulers of Campania and Sicily from the 10th till the late 13th centuries. From 1530 till 1798 the taro was a silver coin, worth a fifth of a **ducat**, or a twelfth of a **scudo**, issued by the Knights of Malta.

Tenga   Variant of **denga**, denoting the unit of currency used at Bokhara in Soviet Central Asia, 1921.

Ternar   Medieval Polish coin worth 3 **pfennigs** or **denars**, derived from the Latin *ternarius* (threefold). Ternars were minted in the 14th–16th centuries and were tariffed variously at 2 to the **schilling**, 4 to the **groschen** or 180 to the **gulden**.

Testone   Italian silver coin, deriving its name from the word *testa* (head), first minted at Milan by the Sforzas in 1474. It was the Milanese counterpart of the **lira** issued by Nicola Tron in Venice two years earlier and was worth 240 **denari** imperiali. It was the prototype for a wide range of large silver coins copied in other Italian cities and eventually elsewhere in Europe: the *teston* of France and Lorraine, the *testoon* of Scotland and the *tester* or **shilling** in England.

Tetartemorion   Greek for quarter, the name given to the tiny quarter **obol**, originally struck in silver but from the 3rd century B.C. in bronze.

Tetarteron   Byzantine gold coin introduced by Nice-phorous Phocas in the 10th century, by devaluing the **solidus** by 8 per cent. In the 11th century it decreased in weight and value and under the late Byzantine rulers degenerated to a coin in billon or copper.

Tetradrachm   Greek word for four **drachmae**, denoting silver coins struck in many parts of the Greek world from the 6th century B.C. and eventually copied by mints as far afield as Syracuse and Thrace.

Tetrobol   Silver coin worth 4 **obols** or two-thirds **drachma**, struck in many parts of Greece down till the 2nd century B.C., and particularly associated with the Achaean League (280–146 B.C.).

Thebe   Unit of currency in Botswana since 1966 when it made its debut as a 10-thebe gold coin. Circulating coins adopted in 1976 were retariffed at 100 thebe to the **pula** or **rand** and were struck in aluminium (1t.), bronze (5t.) or cupro-nickel (10 and 25t.).

Third-Guinea   British gold coin worth 7 **shillings**, introduced in 1797 to relieve the shortage of silver during the Napoleonic Wars and minted till 1813.

Thistle crown   English gold coin worth 4 **shillings** introduced in 1604 and deriving its name from the crowned thistle on the reverse. The use of the heraldic emblems of England and Scotland and the Latin motto *Tueatur Unita Deus* (May God protect the United) reflect the propaganda nature of this coin, issued soon after the union of the crowns.

Thistle merk   Silver coin worth 13s 4d **sterling**, issued as the principal unit of the eighth coinage of James VI of Scotland from 1601 to 1604. Half, quarter and eighth thistle merks were also issued. The name was derived from the crowned thistle on the reverse.

Thistle noble   Gold coin worth 11 **merks** or 14s 8d **sterling**, issued in 1588 as the fifth coinage of James VI of Scotland. The obverse was based on that of the English **noble**, but had the lion of Scotland superimposed.

Threefarthings, Threehalfpence   Small silver coins issued in 1561–82 to provide a greater range of small change in Elizabethan England. These coins, together with the threepence and sixpence, bore no notation of value but were distinguished from the halfpenny, penny, twopence and groat by having a rose inserted behind the queen's effigy on the obverse. Silver threehalfpences were minted as late as 1862 for circulation in British colonies (British Guiana, Ceylon and Jamaica).

Threepence   First minted as a silver coin in England in 1551, it continued in this form until 1944, though the last dates (1942–4) were intended for colonial use only. It was gradually superseded from 1937 onwards by a twelve-sided coin in nickel brass and this continued till 1967, being demonetised in 1970. Silver threepences were also minted for use in Australia, South Africa, New Zealand and other Commonwealth countries. Nickel or cupro-nickel three-pences, inscribed in Gaelic *leat-reul* (half real), were issued in the Irish Free State (later the Republic of Ireland) from 1928 till 1968.

Thrymsa   Early Anglo-Saxon gold coin based on the Merovingian **tremissis** or third-**solidus**, current in Kent, London and York about A.D. 630–75.

Tical   Unit of weight in Thailand, first appearing as coins, in the form of crudely shaped bullet money current from the 14th till the late 19th centuries. Coins minted in Europe date from 1860 and consisted of six silver pieces from 2 ticals to 1/16 tical. These subdivisions had distinctive names: 32 **solot** = 16 **atts** = 8 **peinung** or **sio** = 4 **songpy** or **sik** = 2 **fuang** = 1 **salung**; 4 **salungs** = 1 **tical**. The currency was decimalised in 1909 (100 **satangs** = 1 tical), and the tical was superseded by the **baht** about 1950.

Tien   Small copper coin, formerly used in Annam and subsequently in Vietnam.

Tin   Metallic element, chemical symbol *St (Stannum)*. Because of its unstable nature and tendency to oxidise badly when exposed to the atmosphere, it is unsatisfactory as a coinage metal, but has been used on several occasions, not-ably in Malaya, Thailand, and the East Indies. Tin was also used for British halfpence and farthings, 1672–92.

Toea   Unit of currency in Papua New Guinea since 1975 (100 = 1 *kina*). Bronze 1 and 2, and cupro-nickel 5, 10 and 20 toea have been issued.

Token   Any piece of money whose nominal value is greater than its intrinsic value is, strictly speaking, a token or promise. Thus most of the coins issued since 1914 can be regarded in this light, but numismatists reserve the term for pieces of limited validity and circulation produced by tradesmen, chambers of commerce and other organisations during times of a shortage of government coinage. The term is also loosely applied to metal tickets of admission, such as **Communion tokens,** or **jetons** and **counters** intended for games of chance. Tokens with a nominal value may be produced for security reasons to lessen the possibility of theft from vending machines, telephones, parking meters and transport facilities. Tokens exchangeable for goods have been issued by cooperative societies and used in prisons and internment camps in wartime. In addition to the traditional coinage alloys, tokens have been produced in ceramics, plastics, wood and stout card in circular, square or polygonal shapes.

Tola   Indian unit of weight (11.6g.) used till the early 20th century in bullion transactions. Ingots and tokens cast or struck in .995 fine gold were widely used as currency by merchants, banks and finance companies, many different designs being used.

Toman   Gold unit adopted by Persia (Iran) in 1794 for bullion transactions and later as **money of account** on par with the Indian **mohur,** worth 10 silver **krans.** Gold coins in denominations from one-fifth to 10 tomans were issued between 1896 and 1925.

Tombac   Type of brass alloy with a high copper content, used in coinage requiring a rich golden colour. It is, in fact, a modern version of the *aurichalcum* used by the Romans. It was used for the Canadian 5-cent coins of 1942–3, while the 5- and 10-pfennig coins of Germany have a tombac cladding on a steel core.

Tornese   Italian coin modelled on the **gros tournois** of the late 15th century, but struck in billon instead of silver. Copper tornesi were issued by Naples, 1560–1860. 200 tornesi = 1 **ducato.**

Tostao   Portuguese silver coin, based on the **testone,** introduced in the early 16th century.

Touchpiece   Coin kept as a lucky charm, but more specifically the medieval gold **angel** of England which was worn round the neck as an antidote to scrofula, otherwise known as king's evil from the belief that the reigning monarch possessed the power of healing. The ceremony of touching for king's evil involved the suspension of an angel round the victim's neck, hence the prevalence of these coins pierced for suspension.

Tournois   Adjective denoting the French city of Tours whose weights were adopted as standard throughout France and whose **deniers** and **gros** became the model for medieval French coinage. From the denier and gros tournois came such coins as the **tornese** of Italy and the **turner** of Scotland.

Trade dollar   Large silver pieces minted by Britain, the United States, the Netherlands, and Japan to compete with the Spanish, and later the Mexican, **peso** or 8-**reales** as trade coins in the Far East in the late 19th and early 20th centuries.

Transport tokens   Coin-like pieces of metal, plastic or card issued by companies and corporations to employees and exchangeable for rides on municipal transport systems, date from the mid-19th century. In more recent times similar tokens have been used in many countries to activate turnstiles in buses, trams and subway systems.

Treasure trove   Legal term for coin, bullion, gold or silver articles found hidden in the earth, for which no owner can be discovered. The medieval right of the ruler to buried treasure is now vested in the state. The finder is required to report the matter to the coroner but receives the full market value of any articles or coins retained by the state. Similar laws exist in most countries, except India where the finder receives three-quarters and the owner of the land a quarter of the net value.

Treasury note   Paper money worth 10 **shillings** or £1 issued by the British Treasury on the outbreak of the First World War when **specie** payments were suspended, and continuing till 1928 when the Bank of England took over responsibility for note-issuing. They were popularly known as

"Bradburys" from the signature of the Treasury official engraved on them.

Tremissis   Roman gold coin worth a third of a **solidus**, introduced in the early 5th century. It was used extensively in the Byzantine Empire, as well as by the Lombards, Visigoths and Franks in the Dark Ages, and served as the model for the Anglo-Saxon **thrymsa**.

Tressis   Late Roman coin worth 3 **asses**, struck at many of the provincial mints.

Tressure   Ornamental border framing the field of a coin.

Tridrachm   Silver coin worth 3 **drachmae** minted at Rhodes and Corinth and respectively worth an Aegnietan **didrachm** and a **stater**.

Triens   Latin for third, denoting a bronze coin in the **Aes grave** series worth a third of an **as** or 4 **unciae**.

Trihemiobol   Small silver coin worth 1½ **obols** or a quarter **drachma**, issued by Athens and other states in central Greece in the 4th century B.C.

Triobol   Silver coin worth 3 **obols** or half a **drachma**, extensively minted in ancient Greece.

Tritartemorion   Greek for three-quarter part, signifying the three-quarter **obol** silver coin of ancient Greece.

Troy weight   System of weights derived from the French town of Troyes whose standard pound was adopted in England in 1526. It continued in Britain till 1879 when it was abolished, with the exception of the troy ounce and its decimal parts and multiples, which were retained for gold, silver, platinum and precious stones. The troy ounce of 480 grains is used by numismatists for weighing coins.

Truncation   Stylised cut at the base of a coinage effigy, sometimes containing the die number, engraver's initials or **mint mark**.

Trussel   Reverse die in **hammered** coinage, the opposite of the **pile**.

Tugrik (tughrik)   Mongolian currency unit (= 100 mongo), issued originally as a silver coin (1925) but struck in aluminium bronze or cupro-nickel since 1971.

Turner   Scottish copper coin worth 2-pence, introduced by James VI in 1604 and last minted in 1697. The name is derived from the French **tournois**.

Twopence (tuppence)   Small silver coin worth half a **groat**, introduced in England in 1351 and minted for general circulation till 1786, though surviving to this day as part of the **Maundy** series. Pure copper coins of this value, weighing 2 ounces and appropriately nicknamed **cartwheels** were issued in 1797. Bronze coins of 2 new pence have been struck since 1971.

Type   Principal motif on a coin or medal, enabling numismatists to identify the issue.

U

Uncia   Latin for ounce, signifying a twelfth of a Roman **pound** or a bronze coin worth a twelfth of an **as** in the **Aes grave** series.

Uncirculated   Term used in grading coins to denote specimens in perfect condition, with original mint lustre. In recent years the term "Brilliant Uncirculated" has been adopted (abbreviated as B. Unc. or B.U.).

Unicorn   Scottish gold coin named after the national emblem on the observe. It was introduced in 1484, struck in 21 carat gold and worth 18 **shillings**. Half unicorns were added under James IV (1488–1513), but under James V (1513–42) the unicorn was raised to 20s and then to 22s, but was last minted in 1526.

Uniface   Coin, medal or token with a device on one side only.

Union Latin   see **Latin Monetary Union.**

Unit   Scottish gold coin worth £12 Scots (£1 sterling), struck at Edinburgh, 1604–42 as the counterpart of the English **unite.**

Unite   English gold coin introduced in 1604 as a quasi-propaganda piece to strengthen the ties between Scotland and England following the accession of James VI and I. Unites were struck at the Tower mint till 1648, but triple unites, unites and half unites were produced by the Royalists in a number of towns under their control during the Civil War.

V

Veld Pond   Dutch for "field pound", denoting gold coins struck by the Boer guerrillas at Pilgrims Rest in 1902 in imitation of the British **sovereign**.

Vellon   see **Billon**

Venezolano   Unit of currency in Venezuela, 1876–9 (= 100 **centavos**). Coins worth 10 **reales** were struck in .835 fine silver, being superseded by the **bolivar** of 5 reales in .900 fine silver.

Vereinstaler   German for Convention or Union **taler**, alluding to the Austro-German Monetary Union founded in 1857, providing for the minting of 60 talers to the kilogram of fine silver. Coins of this standard were struck by many of the German states till 1872.

Verrechnungscheine   German for "reckoning notes", denoting the **scrip** issued to German troops prior to the invasion of a country, and exchanged for that country's currency when the invasion was completed.

Victoriate   Small silver coin worth a **drachma**, issued by Rome during the Second Punic War, and deriving its name from the winged figure of Victory on the reverse.

Vintem   Portuguese word for twenty, signifying the 20-**reis** silver coin of 1489–1557, and also a copper coin of Brazil from the 17th–19th centuries.

Virenium   Alloy of copper, nickel and zinc with a magnetic element used for high-denomination coins struck by the Pobjoy Mint. The name is derived from Virena Pobjoy, wife of the mint's chairman.

W

Wampum   Barter currency of the North American Indians, composed of shells of *Venus mercenaria* strung together to form belts or "fathoms", worth 5 **shillings**. Wampum were tariffed variously from 3 to 6 to the English **penny** in the American colonies till 1704.

Wark   Gold unit of Ethiopia, struck as a series of gold coins from an eighth wark to 4 wark between 1916 and 1931.

White Gold   see **Electrum**

Won   Unit of currency in Korea. 100 **chon** = 1 won (Korean Empire, North Korea); 100 **hwan** (1945–62) or *jeon* (since 1962) = 1 won (South Korea).

Wooden coins   Thin pieces of wood used as tokens are known from the 19th–20th centuries in many parts of China and Africa, and as small **Notgeld** from Austria and Germany during the First World War. Wooden nickels is the somewhat contradictory name given to tokens of a commemorative nature, widely popular in the United States since 1930.

Wood's halfpence   Generic term for token **farthings** and **halfpence** struck by William Wood at Bristol in 1722–3 for circulation in Ireland. They were unpopular there because of their inferior alloy known as **Bath metal**, and were subsequently shipped off to the American colonies where they circulated as small change. They are sometimes known as Hibernia tokens, on account of their reverse motif.

X

Xeraphim   Portuguese colonial coin deriving its name from the seraphim or saints portrayed on its obverse. These coins circulated in Goa, Diu and Damao from 1570 till 1871 and were tariffed at 360 or 300 **reis** (half an Indian **rupee**).

Xu (su)   Unit of currency in French Indochina, equivalent to the **sou**, now used in Vietnam (100 = 1 **hao** or **dong**).

Y

Yang   Korean silver coin, 1892–1902, worth 10 **mun** or 100 **fun**. The 5-yang coin of 1892 was equal to the **trade dollar**.

Yen   Japanese currency unit adopted in 1870 on decimalisation, and worth 100 **sen** or 1,000 **rin**.

Yüan   Chinese silver dollar worth .72 **tael** or 7 **mace** and 2 **candareens**, last minted in 1936. Since 1949, 1 renminbi yüan = 10 **chiao** or 100 fen (People's Republic); 1 yüan = 10 chiao or 100 **cents** (Taiwan).

Yüzlük   Turkish silver coin meaning "hundred piece" and worth 2½ **piastres** or 100 **paras**. It was introduced at the beginning of the 19th century and modelled on the **Maria Theresa taler**.

Z

Zaïre   Unit of currency in Zaïre, formerly Congo (Kinshasa), introduced in 1971 (= 100 **macuta**).

Zecchino   Gold coin deriving its name from the Zecca palace which contained the Venetian mint, and often anglicised as "sequin". These gold pieces were originally on par with the **ducat** and were wisely used in the Levantine trade from 1284 till the abolition of the Venetian Republic in 1797. Gold zecchini were also struck by the Knights of Rhodes and Malta.

Zinc   Metallic element, chemical symbol Zn, widely used, with copper, as a constituent of brass, although it was not isolated till the 18th century. Alloyed with copper to form **tombac,** it was used for Canadian 5-cent coins (1942–3) and coated on steel, was used for American cents (1943). Zinc was used for **emergency coinage** in Austria, Belgium, Luxembourg and Germany (1915–18) and in Germany and German-occupied countries during the Second World War. Since then alloys of copper, nickel and zinc have been used for coinage in eastern Europe, and an alloy of zinc with titanium is now being developed as a durable but cheaper substitute for bronze.

Zloty (plural **zlote, zlotych**)   Polish word for gold, hence the name given to the **ducats** introduced in 1528 under Sigismund I. Zlotys in both gold and silver were minted under Russian rule. The zloty was adopted as the currency unit of the Polish Republic (1924), divided into 100 **groszy**.

Zolotoj   Russian for gold, hence the alternative name given to the **elisabeth d'or** or 10 **rouble** gold piece of 1755–9.

Zweidritteltaler   Large silver coin worth two-thirds of an imperial **taler,** minted by many central and north German principalities from the late 17th century till about 1750.

Zyfert   Small billon coin of East Friesland worth half a **stuiver,** issued from the late 16th century till about 1800.